Berkshire
MURDERS

JOHN VAN DER KISTE

The History Press

First published 2010

The History Press
The Mill, Brimscombe Port
Stroud, Gloucestershire, GL5 2QG
www.thehistorypress.co.uk

British Library Cataloguing in Publication Data.
A catalogue record for this book is available from the British Library.

ISBN 978 0 7509 5129 6

Typesetting and origination by The History Press
Printed in India by Nutech Print Services

CONTENTS

AUTHOR'S NOTE & ACKNOWLEDGEMENTS

During the last three or four centuries Berkshire has witnessed a number of violent killings as savage and appalling, or occasionally downright tragic, as anywhere else in England. There were cases where the murderer committed suicide, one of these involving a widower who poisoned his children (one of whom survived) before doing the same to himself; and a suicide pact which left one partner dead and the other a human wreck, to spend the rest of his life in Broadmoor. There was the murder of a young boy by his insane father; the apparently motiveless slaying of a popular pub landlady by a youth who blamed the influence of 'the pictures', a chilling forerunner of the effect that 'video nasties' would have on a later generation; the death of a young woman at the hands of her husband, exasperated by her infidelities, whose execution was to be immortalised in Oscar Wilde's *The Ballad of Reading Gaol*; and, perhaps worst of all, the story of the woman now remembered as England's most notorious baby farmer.

For the twenty-four chapters in this book, a few minor liberties have been taken with the county boundaries of Berkshire. To take one example, the murder of Ann Pullen in 1833 was committed at Wantage in 'old Berkshire', which, since 1974, has been in Oxfordshire. Conversely, Ann Reville was killed in 1881 in Slough, which was then in Berkshire and is now in Buckinghamshire. I trust readers will accept these small degrees of licence.

Particular thanks are due to my wife Kim for her constant support, encouragement and assistance with reading through the draft manuscript; to Nicola Sly for always being ready with helpful advice and information whenever needed; to Simon Dell MBE; Len Woodley, Berkshire Police Historian of the Police History Society, for special assistance with the Hungerford police murders illustrations; to Mrs Beryl Hedges, Mr R.J. Hunter and Roger Long, for general information; to Kenneth Allen,

Terry Bean, Colin Bates, Dr Neil Clifton, Nigel Cox, Peter Land, Brian Marshall, Andrew Smith and R. Sones for permission to reproduce images of copyrighted material; and, as ever, my editors at The History Press, Matilda Richards and Beth Amphlett, for their continued help and encouragement in seeing the book through to publication.

Every effort has been made to obtain permission to reuse material which may be in copyright, and I would be grateful if any holders of relevant material whose rights may have been inadvertently infringed would notify us, so that a suitable correction can be made to subsequent editions.

John Van der Kiste, 2010

1

THE GIBBET ON
INKPEN HILL

Combe, 1676

One of Berkshire's earliest murders took place during the late seventeenth century. Many of the facts are now obscured by the mists of antiquity, but the most commonly given version of events is as follows.

George Broomham, a farmer at West Woodhay, began an affair with Dorothy Newman, a widow who lived at nearby Combe. George was already married, and Martha was a faithful wife, but he had tired of her and fell prey to the charms of Mrs Newman. Divorce in those days was almost unheard of, especially for those outside the nobility who could never even contemplate the expense of such an action. The only way to dispose of an unwanted spouse was by arranging for his or her death, while trying to make it look accidental.

While coming home from work one day, George noticed a wasps' nest, realised that this would help him to commit what he believed would be the perfect crime, and made a mental note of the location. A few days later, husband and wife went to market together, and he mentioned the nest. Martha was keen to see it, so George pulled up his pony and trap, and they got out together to have a look. As they did so, George put on a pair of thick leather gauntlets, saying he needed them to pull the brambles aside on their way. While Martha looked at the nest, he crept up behind her, seized her by the shoulders and forced her head into the nest. Taken by surprise, she did not even scream, and as they were miles away from anywhere or anyone else, there would have been no point in trying to raise the alarm. Martha tried to struggle, but her husband was too strong for her, and it was only a matter of time before she was stung to death.

Feeling satisfied with having stage-managed what appeared to be a dreadful accident, George returned to his cart and proceeded on to market. The next day

The seventeenth-century Combe gibbet at Inkpen Hill.
(© Brian Robert Marshall)

Martha's body was found, and George had no difficulty in playing the role of a grief-stricken widower.

George came close to getting away with murder, but, according to one source, the next time he visited Dorothy Newman, he told her the full story as they sat in her cottage, and were overheard by her son, who pretended to be asleep. The next day he repeated everything to the authorities, who arrested George and took him to Winchester Gaol.

Another version of the story says that both lovers were involved in the killing of Martha Broomham and that she was in fact beaten to death, probably with a staff. They had believed they were alone, but they were seen by the village idiot, 'Mad Thomas', who went and told the magistrates what he had seen. Yet another version suggests that Robert, the young son of George and Martha, was also killed on the Downs, as his father was determined that nobody would stand in the way of his love affair with Dorothy.

Whatever the truth of the matter, George Broomham was tried and convicted at Winchester Assizes of the wilful murder of his wife on or around 23 February 1676. He was sentenced to be hanged in chains near the site of the murder. Those who say that Dorothy Newman took part in the murder also maintain that she stood in the dock alongside him and shared his fate.

As the murder had been committed on the boundary between the parishes of Combe and Inkpen, there was some dispute as to exactly where the execution should take place, and who would be responsible for making arrangements. The murder scene was on the top of a hill, and there was no nearby tree suitable to provide a gallows, so a gibbet would need to be erected for the purpose. Both parishes said that the spot was outside their boundary, and the other would have to pay for it. The arguments were only brought to an end when the court ruled that a gibbet was to be erected at the site of a Stone-Age long barrow at the top of Inkpen Hill.

From here the body of George Broomham, and perhaps that of his lover, was hung, and left in chains as a deterrent to others until the bones had bleached with age and exposure to sunlight.

Ironically, in view of the trouble the gibbet had caused, it was never to be used again for carrying out a death sentence. Even so, its presence became a much-hallowed local landmark. When the wooden post rotted away it was replaced with a second grisly tourist attraction. The second one was destroyed by lightning, and opportunists removed the fragments as souvenirs. Further gibbets have been erected on the same spot as each one has fallen victim to severe weather or vandalism. Though no real live, or dead, bodies have been suspended from it, a group of American soldiers stationed in the area during the Second World War are said to have dangled an effigy of Adolf Hitler from the crossbar in 1944.

2

MURDER ON MARKET DAY

Caversham, 1722

Jacob Saunders was born around 1700 at Reading. His father, a woolcomber, was liked and respected as an honest and upright citizen, but from his youth young Jacob always had a reputation for bad behaviour. A cheat and thief, he was the scourge of the neighbourhood, and some people blamed his father for not restraining him properly. All attempts to train him for a proper profession were frustrated by his refusal to work. Instead he spent his time hanging around in the street, when not robbing hen roosts or fruit orchards, sometimes on his own and sometimes with others.

At the age of twenty Jacob married Elizabeth Grey, a furniture repairer and upholsterer. If his father had hoped that the young man might now settle down and make something of himself, he was soon to be disappointed. Jacob's crimes were about to progress from mere thieving to something much more serious.

One Saturday market day in the autumn of 1722, Mr Blagrave, a farmer who lived just outside Reading, brought a large quantity of corn to sell for about £60. Being an inquisitive soul, Saunders soon found out. He had long kept an eye on the regular market traders, hoping to make some easy money. As a result, he was aware that Blagrave was one of the farmers who tended not to hurry home straight afterwards, but usually stayed behind to have a drink or two and chat with the others, and Jacob decided to shadow him for the rest of the day. True to form, after the close of business Blagrave went to join his friends for a noggin at the Catherine Wheel pub nearby. Jacob kept his distance, but had decided he would follow him home over the fields afterwards. The unsuspecting Blagrave noticed him coming in to sit at the inn, and exchanged a few friendly words with him.

It was approaching midnight when Blagrave left to go home. He walked across the meadows to Caversham, about a mile away, without any suspicion that the man he had struck up a brief conversation with earlier was keeping a discreet but close distance behind him. As they passed through the village Saunders took a large club out of a baker's woodstack, and once they had gone through Caversham he increased his pace till he caught up with Blagrave. Just as the latter was crossing a stile, the younger man struck him on the head, laid him flat on the ground, and continued to beat him with the club until he was sure he was dead. Even then, Jacob was afraid to search through Blagrave's pockets till he had pulled off his own garters and bound his victim hand and foot.

To his disappointment, he found only a shilling and some halfpence in the farmer's jacket and trousers. All he could do in his frustration was to abuse the bruised, mangled and, as he thought, dead body a little more, which he did by beating it again with his club and stamping upon it with his feet. He then went home to bed, not speaking a word of the day's events to his wife, who nevertheless found his behaviour distinctly strange.

Blagrave was not yet dead. He lay, bruised and helpless, until he was found early the next morning by some who recognised him. They carried him back to his house and sent for the surgeons immediately. Though his constitution was very strong and it was thought he might still live for several days, there could be no hope for him. Until his death, a day or two later, he never recovered enough to give any account of his misfortune, which would have been enough to identify the perpetrator.

Yet Saunders had been noticed at the inn at the same time as Blagrave. As both had left at roughly the same time, this was enough to make him a wanted man. That same day a few people in the town decided to watch out for him. Unusually, they saw him going to church, where they thought he looked 'more heavy and dull than usual, though he had always a downward countenance, almost sufficient to have informed people what he was.'

Caversham.

While he was attending divine service a deputation went to the Mayor, told him of their suspicions, and gave him details of everything they had noticed and heard. The Mayor issued a warrant for Saunders' arrest and sent officers to seize him as he came out of church and take him to gaol. A separate warrant was made out for his wife, so that she could also be questioned. She was put into a different cell in the same prison, so they would have no contact and no chance to arrange an alibi for him.

That evening the Mayor and some of his men visited them both. On being questioned for the first time Saunders strongly denied having killed anyone, but his answers seemed rather confused and he convinced nobody. His wife, who evidently saw no reason to become implicated in his misdoings, made no attempt to deny that he had come home unusually late, and somewhat dishevelled. When she was shown the garters with which Blagrave's hands had been bound, she admitted that they belonged to her husband. Both of them were detained in custody pending further questioning.

That night Jacob escaped from prison and returned to his father's house, where he was discovered trying to hide. By the time he was interrogated again, he realised it was useless to deny it any longer, confessed to the murder, and told the officers where to find the club with which he had battered Mr Blagrave. They found it at once, and Saunders was committed to the county gaol.

He made one last futile effort to avoid the inevitable. According to criminal law, when two or three people were suspected of any felony or murder, the one that informed on the others would be reprieved from execution. With this in mind, Jacob tried to implicate two other local men of bad reputation whom the community would have believed might have been equally guilty, and swore an affidavit against them before the authorities. Both men were arrested on suspicion of murder and gaoled for several weeks that winter. Nevertheless, they were able to prove their innocence, and after being tried at Reading Assizes in March 1723 they were acquitted.

Two days later Jacob was escorted to Oxford under heavy guard, where he was sentenced to be hung in chains at the spot where he had attacked Blagrave. As this was near Caversham, the villagers asked if his execution could be carried out instead on the heath four miles away at the suitably named Gallows Tree Common, where a tree stood with one arm growing into another, forming the likeness of a gallows. The gibbet was accordingly erected there and on Monday 15 March 1723, Jacob Saunders was executed, and then hung up in irons.

3

THE WHITE HART MURDER

Wantage, 1833

On 30 August 1833, nineteen-year-old George King, an itinerant fruit picker, was working at Court Hill Farm, near Wantage. Early in the evening he finished his bean-cutting duties and stopped for a drink at the Squirrel Inn, Grove Street, on the way back to his lodgings at the White Hart in Newbury Street. The landlady at the latter was forty-year-old Ann Pullen, a widow, who had a daughter aged six and a stepson, James, aged twelve. As he walked in, Mrs Pullen cut him a rasher of bacon, which he put on the end of his knife to cook over the log fire, and she then served him a mug of ale. After his supper, he went out to the yard to use the lavatory, and when he came back she bolted the door for the night.

At this point, he seized his bean cutter, grabbed her, and cut her throat until he had severed her head from her body. Next he took the blade to her apron pocket containing her purse, removed the keys to the inn from her belt, and let himself out of the premises. King headed straight to the Blue Boar, almost directly opposite. His plan was presumably to establish an alibi by posing as an innocent labourer going about his lawful business, prior to returning to his lodgings, and then finding the body of his landlady who had been murdered in his absence. He entered the Blue Boar at about 9.45 p.m., and although it was raining outside, he had his coat doubled up on his arm. This immediately aroused the suspicions of William Betteridge, the landlord, who wondered why the man was not wearing it, and whether he was trying to conceal something.

King went to the bar and ordered a pint of beer, dropping a large amount of cash on the bar and paying a halfpenny for the drink. Betteridge then noticed that although King was carrying the coat over his arm, he was not very wet, and had presumably not been outside for long. Next, King asked if he could have a bed for the night. The landlady told him they had no rooms left, but perhaps he would find one available if he made enquiries from Mrs Pullen at the White Hart opposite. Leaving the bar, he took his beer over to some other patrons at a nearby table and offered it to them as he no longer wanted it. Next he offered to play anybody in the room at skittles, maybe in a half-hearted attempt to ingratiate himself with the regulars. However, Mr Betteridge intended to close shortly and said it was too late for any more games.

There were about five other customers left at this time. One was a young Frenchman, Charles Marriot, employed by a local blacksmith. He was sitting on his own when King went over to him, said he had no shelter for the night, and hoped to find somewhere to stay at Hanney, four miles north of Wantage. If Marriot would agree to accompany King on the journey, he would pay Marriot one shilling, but the latter took one look at King's bean hook and wisely declined the offer. Then King asked if Marriot would help him find another tavern for the night, to which he agreed.

They walked out of the inn at closing time into the dark, wet night, hurried past the White Hart, and found all the other inns were shut. Marriot must have taken pity on King, or possibly feared that to antagonize this man with his ferocious weapon would be asking for trouble, so he agreed to let him share a space for the night at a nearby stable in Back Street. King paid him 6d for the privilege, and proceeded to make Marriot pay dearly for it with a night of mumbling, thrashing about and threats to hang himself. Marriot was given little chance to sleep properly and must have considered the money well earned by the time morning came. King set off on the road to Hanney, stopping on the way to do some work at Court Farm.

Meanwhile, Ann Pullen's children were about to make the dreadful discovery of her headless body as they came downstairs to the kitchen at the White Hart. James and his friend Tom ran to fetch family and friends, who in turn fetched the police and the local surgeon, Henry Osmond. Word soon spread about what had happened, and villagers came to try and take a look at the macabre scene, while Constable Thomas Jackson attempted to keep them from interfering with the crime scene. Dr Osmond examined the body, and was sure that the beheading had been done by a single powerful blow from a sharp blade, severing the neck at the second vertebra. It had been carried out cleanly, not with an axe or a kitchen knife, but with an instrument with a finely-honed blade like a pea or bean hook, which would cut cleanly through the bone.

The coroner, Edward Cowcher, arrived about noon, after calling for a jury for an immediate inquest into the death. Accompanied by Thomas Goodlake, the county magistrate, they viewed the body and spoke with Dr Osmond. It did not take long for suspicion to fall on King, who had been seen by Tom Gregory as he entered the White Hart at about 9 p.m. the previous night. Others confirmed that between thirty and forty minutes later he was seen in the Blue Boar 'in an agitated state'. Two men were already implicated, King and Marriot, as they had been seen setting off together late the previous night from the Blue Boar.

King was apprehended that morning while he was working in the bean field. Mr Crane, a fellow labourer, asked King where his coat was. King said it was under a bean sheaf in the field where he had been working, and he volunteered to fetch it. Instead Crane went to collect it, and found it covered in blood, with a woman's purse containing 12s and a bent 6d piece inside. This was Ann Pullen's lucky sixpence, which she always carried around with her – though possession of it had sadly not been proof against the worst luck of all. King was formally arrested by Constable James Jones and taken into custody. Marriott was also apprehended as a suspect, but William Betteridge of the Blue Boar explained the connection between the men, and confirmed that they were not partners in crime. Marriot explained that King had offered him 6d to stay with him, and that King 'appeared to be in a fidget and said he was going to hang himself.'

Having failed to place the blame on his newly-found companion, King invented a suspect. He told the inquest that he had gone to the White Hart with Edward Grant, a labourer from Reading who had been working with him, and who went in and struck off Mrs Pullen's head with a single blow. Magistrates sent messengers to try and locate Mr Grant, but on their return they reported that no such man was in the area. There was no such person.

Mrs Pullen's lucky sixpence had been identified by Wantage washerwoman Rachael Sandford and her friend Eliza Clench, while the blood on King's clothes and his irrational, restless behaviour on the night of the murder in the Blue Boar, were mentioned by several witnesses.

One might have expected some decorum to be shown by Ann Pullen's mother, while her daughter lay dead in her home. Instead, she and other members of the family saw fit to profit from the tragedy by taking advantage of the trade in sightseeing. Those who wished to come and look at the corpse of her headless daughter were organised into a paying queue, allowed to pass through the back kitchen and into the street and see as much as they wanted, for a small consideration. It was a display which the local papers fiercely condemned, calling the family 'utterly callous to all sense of decency'.

On 2 September, at the inquest, King had abandoned all hope of placing the blame on the fictitious Grant. Instead he tried to incriminate Marriot, but all the evidence made it plain that the latter was completely innocent. In the afternoon the jury returned a verdict of wilful murder against King, and he was committed for trial at the Reading Assizes in February 1834. Ann Pullen's funeral was held the following day, thus putting an end to the abhorrent peepshow organised by her mercenary mother.

Spectators now had another sight for their morbid curiosity – that of George King being placed in the police cart on his way to Reading Gaol. On the journey, he confessed his crime to Constable Jackson. He said he had meant to hit Ann Pullen with the back of the hook, and after administering the blow, he fell back against the parlour door, as if somebody had lifted him. Her eyes had then quivered, and

The Trial & Confession of Geo: King

For the Diabolical Murder of Ann Pullen,

LANDLADY OF THE WHITE HART, WANTAGE,

BY CUTTING OFF HER HEAD with a BEAN-HOOK,

AND WHO WAS ORDERED FOR

EXECUTION

MONDAY, MARCH 3, 1834.

"Thou shalt do no murder." Matthew, ch. xix. v. 18.

"Whoso sheddeth man's blood, by man shall his blood be shed." Genesis, ch. ix. v. 6.

THE trial of the above wretched man took place at Reading, on Thursday, Feb. 27, 1834, before Mr. Justice Patterson. The prisoner appeared a very heavy-looking, clumsy young man; and displayed a perfect indifference when placed at the bar.

It appeared that the deceased was a widow, living in Wantage, where she kept the White Hart Public House; her family consisting of two children, the eldest of them 12 years old.

On the 30th of August last, the eldest child, a boy, was sent to bed about nine o'clock; and, on the next morning, when he got up, he found the headless body of his mother extended on the floor with the detached head lying near the feet. He immediately called for assistance. The prisoner was suspected, and taken into custody; and on his being searched, 12s. 6d was found in his pocket, and a purse. Among the silver was a sixpence bent in a curious way, which had belonged to the deceased. The prisoner, at the inquest said, that himself and a man named Grant, had gone to the old woman's house, and that Grant went in and struck off the old woman's head by a single blow, and he described her falling, and the spouting of the blood, and the position of the body, just as was the fact, and he said that he stood at the door. Search was made for Grant, but no such person could be found. The Jury returned a verdict of Wilful Murder against the prisoner. To prove

The Confession,

Thomas Jackson was called. He said—I took the prisoner to the Reading Goal: when we got as far as Streatly, we stopped to bait our horse at the Bull. The prisoner went up to a picture that was there, and he smiled. He said, "she turned her eyes about like that picture, when her head was off," and he turned his own eyes like it. The prisoner joked a good deal about it while our horse was feeding. He said he had done the murder. He said he went to Mrs. Pullen's, and as he was going in doors, there was a man coming out, and another man inside the house drinking, who had a little dog, and seem'd as if he was courting the widow; he drank his beer and went away. The prisoner further said, that Mrs. Pullen cut him a rasher of bacon, which he frizzled on the point of his knife—and after having finished his supper he sat down near the window, his bean-hook and cup being on the table, and that he took up the cup in one hand and the hook in the other, and he hit her with the bean-hook, and cut her head off in a moment. He said he meant to have hit her with the back of the hook; and he said as soon as he had given the blow he felt back against the parlour door, as if some one had lifted him; but he sprang forward again and tore her pocket off, and then took the candle to get out, but could not find the bolt of the door, as he let the candle fall and trod upon it; however, on touching the bolt with his thumb, he got out, and folded the pocket up under his right arm. He said that he washed his hands in the river, and threw the pocket into a pond. I asked him how long it was all about; and he said from a quarter of an hour to 20 minutes. I asked him if there was any blood about him, and he said he never thought to look, but that there was a little on the hook when he began to work the next morning, but the dew very soon washed it off.

James Jones the younger said—I was with the last witness. The prisoner said that he frizzled a rasher of bacon on his knife, and proposed to Mrs. Pullen to pass the night with her, whereupon she said she would give him a knock on the head with a poker. That he then left the house for a short time, and on his return, he took up his bean-hook, and had her head off momentarily. He said t was not much of a blow.

The Jury immediately returned a verdict of Guilty.

Mr. Justice Patteson, in a solemn manner, passed sentence of death upon the prisoner, and ordered him for execution.

On Monday, March 3, he suffered his dreadful sentence: owing to the shortness of fall, he struggled violently some minutes, then gave a convulsive shudder, and died. He was a native of Cumnor, Oxfordshire, and was 19, the day of execution. His body was placed in a hole in one of the spare wards of the prison, without the least ceremony.

COPY of VERSES.

GIVE ear ye tender Christians all, and listen unto me,
While I relate a deed of blood, and great barbarity;
A murder of the blackest dye I now repeat in rhyme,
That was committed by George King, a young man in his prime.

'Twas on a Friday evening, he called at the White Hart,
And there he eat and drank, until it was quite dark,
Altho' the worthy landlady did treat him very kind,
To rob and murder her, he most wickedly design'd.

'Twas then he took his bean-hook, and with a dreadful oath,
He sever'd the head from her body with one fearful stroke,
He rifled then her pockets, and took all it did contain,
From off the ghastly body which he'd so vilely slain.

O then his guilty conscience most bitterly did him haunt,
And suspicion falling on him, he was to justice brought,
And then he stood his trist, and by the laws decree
This morning he'll die in scorn upon the fatal tree.

seemed to fix their gaze on him. He also admitted that he had asked her to spend the night with him, but she threatened to hit him on the head with a poker, and, rather lamely, he claimed that when he severed her head with the bean hook, it was 'not much of a blow', as if somehow seeking to excuse his action. He also asked the police officers to write to his father explaining what he had done.

The trial opened on 27 February 1834 before Mr Justice Patterson. Despite having made a full confession, King pleaded not guilty to the charge of murder. Among those giving evidence was the murdered woman's stepson, James. He told the court that he and his sister had gone to bed at about 8 or 9 p.m. on the evening of 30 August, and his mother generally retired at about 10 p.m. The following morning he got up at around 7 a.m., went downstairs and into the blood-splattered kitchen, where he saw his mother's head lying against the fireplace, and her body towards the door.

The bean hook was produced as a key exhibit, and King glanced at it without showing any emotion. There were no witnesses for the defence, and King made no effort to defend himself. He had been provided with defence counsel, one of whom, Mr Carrington, cross-examined Constable Jones and tried to establish that his client had been threatened. King claimed he had been told that if he did not confess to the murder, a staple would be driven into the door of the White Hart and he would be chained to the dead body all night. It was the first time such a suggestion had been raised, and who had made this threat was never stated.

A final issue raised by the defence was that no evidence had been provided to prove that the deceased was in fact Mrs Ann Pullen, but such a legal technicality was ruled out of order by Dr Cowcher.

King was sentenced to be hanged on 3 March. He received the news calmly, without any display of emotion. His mother visited him shortly before the sentence was due to be carried out. He went to the gallows at midday with, in the words of a reporter, 'the same sullen indifference which he exhibited during his trial up to the moment of his execution.' The bolts were pulled, but the fall was too short and he suffered slow strangulation, thrashing and struggling for some minutes before the final convulsive shudder.

When his body was cut down after being left suspended for the customary hour, his head was shaved ready for burial and a description was written down for the files. A large fracture about three-quarters of an inch wide and five inches long was revealed on his skull. According to his mother, it was the result of a fall from a hayloft. This blow to the head, it was thought, could have resulted in mental derangement, leading to this apparently motiveless murder.

4

THE FATAL TRIANGLE

Warfield, 1851

In the 1840s John Carey was well known as the landlord of the Leathern Bottle, off Bracknell Road at Warfield. It was a small but thriving inn, which did a reasonable trade among the locals. During the day John ran the adjoining farm, while his wife, Hannah, took care of the inn. When evening came, she saw to the family meals and looked after their two children, eleven-year-old Alexander and four-year-old Charles, while her husband worked behind the bar. They were a popular and well-liked family.

The couple would doubtless have continued to lead this contented life for years to come had it not been for the appearance of George Parker. He was known locally as a cheerful, good-looking, hardworking farm labourer who enjoyed dropping into the pub for a drink or two, and John and Hannah both regarded him as a friend. Everything was fine until his wife died suddenly after a short illness. George was desolate, and took to drinking heavily. Sorely in need of consolation and company, particularly of the female kind, he found the landlady of the Leathern Bottle genuinely sympathetic to his plight.

Aged thirty-two, Hannah Carey was some fifteen years younger than her husband. At first she merely provided a ready ear when George Parker needed it, but one thing led to another and before long she too had started drinking more than usual, knocking back gin at an alarming rate while Parker sat with her and drank his beer. She seemed much more short-tempered than before, particularly with the boys. They and their father were no longer getting their meals regularly, and John often had to cook his own food after returning from a hard day's work on the farm. Moreover, he found that Hannah was becoming increasingly distant with him. It was painfully clear that she had found something of a kindred spirit in the young, rugged widower.

John Carey was a patient man, and he put up with this state of affairs for four or five years. He dreaded losing Hannah to Parker, and hoped that she would soon tire of her infatuation with him. Unfortunately, it developed into something more, and she became less and less discreet about their relationship. One day John implored her to forsake Parker, so they could return to the happy family life which they had known before he came into their lives. Her reaction was to ask him for an allowance of 8s a week so that she could leave him and their sons and set up home with Parker. Horrified at her blunt statement, which showed that their marriage was dead in all but name, John wept bitterly and begged her to reconsider, but it was in vain.

One Sunday evening he decided to make a stand. While he and Hannah were cleaning tankards behind the bar, Parker walked in asked for his usual pint of beer. John asked Parker politely to leave his house for the sake of him and his family and not to come back. Parker said nothing but looked at Hannah, who immediately took Parker's mug from the shelf, filled it with beer and placed it on the counter in front of him. She then turned to John and told him defiantly that while they had beer in the house, Parker was welcome to enjoy it.

John angrily picked up a wooden bucket and threw it at Hannah, hitting her in the groin before it shattered, and walked out without saying anything. Their elder son, Alexander, had appeared and witnessed the scene. Later that night John returned to the inn, and Hannah taunted him for having run away from her lover. At this he laid into her, kicking her and hitting her with his fists until he could fight no more. She put up little resistance; far from it, she seemed to be urging him on, taunting him as a feeble old good-for-nothing. Her only attempt to ward him off was when she picked up an axe, which they used for cutting firewood, wielded it around in front of his face, and threatened to cut his head off.

From this point on relations between husband and wife went from bad to worse. Parker might have helped to ease the situation if he had done the decent thing and taken his custom elsewhere. However, he continued to drink at the inn, though he did at least do so when he knew John would be out working on the farm or in the fields. Hannah was regularly seen in the public bar with one or both eyes blackened after an altercation with her husband. She continued to threaten to leave him, asking for money so she would have enough to live with Parker.

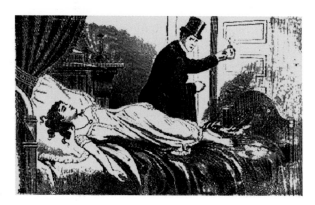

John and Hannah Carey.

After John had attacked her again and left her badly bruised, Hannah took to her bed, refusing all food and drink. John suspected that Parker was still visiting her while his back was turned, something his wife made no effort to deny. Such a situation was clearly untenable for long, and one evening he decided the time had come to resolve matters once and for all. On 21 October 1851, after a long day's work outside, he came upstairs to find Hannah lying in bed. She turned her face to the wall, and refused to speak to him. He told her to get up and go – and never come back.

When she continued to ignore him, he repeated himself, saying this was her last chance to leave of her own free will. Enraged by her continued silence, he snapped. He seized the bed, tore the mattress off the frame and threw Hannah onto the floor. He then hurled the pieces of broken bed on top of her and jumped up and down on them while she struggled. Being quite a heavy man, and with his feet still in hob-nailed, steel toe-capped boots, the damage he did to her was considerable. She screamed as she tried to break free, but to no avail.

Charles had been asleep in the adjoining bedroom, but the noise woke him up and he ran to his mother. She took him in her arms, hoping his presence would ward off her husband's fury, but John grabbed him, moved him aside and continued to beat Hannah until exhaustion prevented him from doing any more. He collapsed on the floor, stricken with remorse as he held her in his arms, a trickle of blood seeping out of her mouth. Eventually he fell asleep, and she was too weak to push him off. For a moment he probably feared that he had killed her, though it was almost certain that he had never intended to do so.

When he woke the next morning he found that his wife's face was covered with dried blood, but she was still breathing. After getting up, he went to fetch the family doctor, Walter Thompson. Both men met in the street, and John told him that his wife was very sick. When Dr Thompson came to examine her, he asked Hannah whether she would like anybody to come and look after her. She said weakly that she would like him to send for her sister, Esther Bruton, from Wokingham. Mrs Bruton came the following day, stayed awhile to try and comfort her badly bruised sister, but knew she could do little more. She reported her sister's condition to John Wigg, the Warfield village constable, and then returned home.

When Hannah's condition deteriorated, Dr Thompson came back with John Westall, a Maidenhead surgeon, for a second opinion. Both men agreed she was dying, and there was nothing more they could do for her. On 5 November Mr Hercy, the local magistrate, came to visit her, bringing Edward Frankum, Clerk to the Justices, to write down her deposition. She began to tell them what had happened, but the effort was too much for her, and before she had a chance to say much, Dr Thompson advised them not to continue the interview as he feared the strain would be too much for her.

On the following day Mrs Bruton returned. Hannah told her she was dying, and asked that after her death her body should be taken to Easthampstead church, where she could rest beside their mother. She also requested that she should take some calico from the cupboard and make some shirts. Esther made a vain effort at trying to cheer her sister up, saying that she would only take the material on condition that she would bring it back once Hannah had recovered.

On 14 November, Hannah gave up the hopeless struggle for life. John Carey was arrested and charged with murder a day later, and Constable Wigg went with him to Reading Gaol. Weeping bitterly, the prisoner said that he never wished to kill his wife, but had acted out of sheer desperation.

On 26 February 1852 he appeared before Mr Justice Baron Platt at Reading Assizes. Evidence was given by Dr Thompson, who had carried out the post-mortem, Mr Westall and Esther Bruton. It was said that Esther had expressed her willingness to travel fifty miles to see her brother-in-law hanged for what he had done to her sister. Dr Thompson said that Mrs Carey's injuries had been very severe. He found the marks of bruises on the lower part of the back, between the shoulders, and all over the legs. There was inflammation of the abdomen, and a large abscess caused by external bruising had formed on one side, enough to cause death. He added that she had led a temperate life until recently, but after she took to drinking heavily she had developed a liver and kidney infection. Mr Westall had assisted at the post-mortem, and said he had never before seen such a severe case of bruising to the abdomen.

Next to take the stand was Mrs Bruton. Although she had not been present at the time and was basing her evidence partly on hearsay, partly on what she imagined had happened, she recounted how Mr Carey had come home in the evening, started to abuse her sister, and snatched their child away from her when she tried to defend herself. She described his throwing the bed and then himself on top of her, and how Hannah's flesh was torn by his boots. One of her toenails, she said, was completely torn away from her right foot. John had left her to suffer, saying that she had not yet been punished enough.

Alexander was also called as a witness, and the judge questioned him as to his mother's drinking habits. The boy said that she drank a lot, especially gin, and he often had to take the bottle away from her when she became intoxicated. He recounted how she would get drunk with Mr Parker, and how his father had often got down on his hands and knees begging her to stop and send Parker away. They had lived very happily until two years earlier, and he had never known them quarrel until Parker came into the house. He often visited, coming after his father had gone out to work, and would stay every day until his mother had gone to bed.

Constable Wigg confirmed that he had known Parker for twenty years. Aged about thirty-five, he was very strong and athletic, much more so than the elder Mr Carey. It was his opinion that the Careys had been very happy together until about four years previously, when Mrs Parker died and George took to frequenting the inn.

Mr John McMahon, counsel for John Carey's defence, said John had gone to summon the doctor for his wife, as well as making the effort to call Mr Westall from Maidenhead. He called into question the medical evidence, which said that the post-mortem had shown she had died from the inflammation or possibly from her bruising, and maintained that if she had suffered liver damage, alcoholic poisoning had been at least partly responsible. In addition, the case was aggravated by the evidence of Mrs Bruton, whose conduct had 'been somewhat remarkable'. Her statement that she would travel fifty miles to see her brother-in-law hang was plainly pejorative, and it would be difficult for the gentlemen of the jury to be too impressed with the statements of any witness who could speak thus in a court of law.

Moreover, he felt it right to draw attention to the fact that when Mr Carey had refused to serve Mr Parker at the inn, his wife had countermanded his instructions by saying that as long as there was beer in the house, Mr Parker should be allowed it. It was hardly surprising that a man who could witness the violation of his domestic relationship, goaded by the treachery of his wife, should on the spur of the moment be driven to commit such an act. After the jury had taken all the facts into consideration, he was sure that members would decide in favour of the prisoner.

In summing up the case, Mr Justice Baron Platt said that with regards to Mrs Carey having said that if John would give her a weekly allowance, she would leave him for Mr Parker, the law of the land protected every man against having to pay the support of his wife when she committed adultery. If she did so, she made herself an outcast, 'and lost altogether to society'. It was therefore for the jury to decide whether the evidence produced before them was such as to convict the prisoner of killing his wife: 'However much he might not intend it, if he did so he renders himself responsible for the act.'

The jury returned a verdict of guilty of murder, but with a recommendation for leniency on the grounds of extreme provocation. Before passing sentence, the judge said that if the injuries had been inflicted in the moment of his wrath, the court might have dealt more leniently with him. However, he had come home one night, and without any aggravation caused his wife's death by dragging her out of bed and trampling on her. There could be no doubt that the injuries she sustained caused her death. It was impossible to allow him to remain in the country, as it would be no deterrent to others if he was given a light punishment. He would be sentenced to transportation for seven years.

John Carey broke down and begged not to be sent out of the country, for the sake of his sons. The judge told him that he felt very much for the children who would now be orphans, but 'I find it impossible I can pass over this.'

5

THE MAD GREAT-UNCLE

Maidenhead, 1852

For many years Isaac Lee was a successful brushmaker in London. He and his wife had enjoyed a happy marriage, and when she died in about 1850 after a short illness he was grief-stricken. After a nervous breakdown, he feared he was losing his mind. In those days there was usually only one destination for those who reached this state, and that was the hospital of St Mary of Bethlehem in London, commonly known as Bedlam, the institution for people regarded to be insane.

Isaac did not regard himself as mad; though once he was in the hospital he feared that if he stayed there much longer he probably would go that way. He wrote to Caroline and John Cannon, his sister and brother-in-law, at Boyn Hill, Maidenhead. As they were the only family he had, he asked if he could go and live with them, offering to contribute £50 a year if they agreed. They considered the idea carefully. As he was financially very well off, and they knew that he would keep his word regarding payment. Yet they were aware that his behaviour could be unpredictable, that he had a violent temper, and sometimes suffered from blackouts. Looking after him would place considerable responsibility on them. However, largely out of genuine concern for his welfare, they agreed to his proposal.

Isaac was therefore released on licence to go and live with them. At first the arrangement worked very well, and the family never wanted for anything. Caroline kept a careful eye on him as much as possible, and ensured that all knives were kept locked away when not in use. Sometimes he was difficult and troublesome, but they managed to deal with him, until his mental condition deteriorated further. On the morning of 16 March 1852, after making sure that Isaac was all right to be on his own for a while, Caroline left the house to go and see a neighbour. John's granddaughter, Lizzie,

The River Thames at Maidenhead.

aged about five, was staying with them at the time. Everything seemed in order until a piglet ran from the yard into the kitchen, evidently looking for some scraps.

For some reason, the sight of the animal turned Isaac into a raging monster. He picked up a large billhook from the floor and brought it down on the animal, snapping its jaw. Squealing in pain, it got to its feet and, with its dying breath, tried to crawl away from him under a shelf. Lizzie came into the kitchen to see what the noise was, took one look at the sight of the bloodstained floor and her wild-eyed great-uncle, screamed in terror, and tried to run from the kitchen. Isaac barred her way, his eyes blazing with anger as he went for her with the billhook as well. Within a few minutes she screamed no longer, and nor did the piglet. Both were lying dead on the floor.

The noise had attracted the attention of neighbours. Appalled at the sight of the carnage, they immediately sent for John and Caroline Cannon, and Lizzie's mother, Eliza. Two constables, Daniel Sexton and Simeon Frewin, were also called. Isaac had calmed down, but when PC Frewin came to arrest him he immediately became violent and excitable, and tried to escape. It took three people to help Frewin get the handcuffs on him.

When Lizzie's body was examined, it was found that in addition to the cuts she had sustained as a result of the billhook, her skull and nose were also broken. It was thought that Isaac must have kicked her or trampled on her body after she was dead. Constable Sexton was so traumatised by what he had witnessed that he was unable to work for a couple of days afterwards.

Isaac Lee was remanded in custody at Reading Gaol, and at the inquest on 17 March the county coroner, Rupert Clark, called an inquest at the Pond House, Boyn Hill. Witnesses were questionned, and the hearing lasted four and a half hours. Neighbours said that when they came on the scene, Lee was as white as a sheet and said he could remember nothing about having attacked the girl or the piglet.

The foreman of the jury said they had no alternative but to record a case of wilful murder. There was no trial, as it was obvious that Lee was unfit to plead. He was sent back to London to spend the rest of his life at Bedlam, the dreaded place from which he had been so grateful to escape.

6

'I CAN'T THINK WHAT I DID IT FOR'

Wokingham, 1856

The cold-blooded murder of a child in a residential area where neighbours know each other well always causes particular revulsion in the community. The one saving grace (if that is the right term) of one such case in the mid-nineteenth century was that the perpetrator was clearly not responsible for his behaviour.

Early in 1855 Mrs Saltmarsh of Bill Hill, two miles from Wokingham, opened a schoolroom. She was very keen to improve the spiritual condition of the poor, and she needed to employ someone as a home missionary, to deliver weekly lectures and sermons to people in the area, and to distribute religious tracts to those who could read. She applied to the London City Mission Society, and on the recommendation of Mr Geldart, the secretary, she employed Charles Forester for the post. In his early thirties, and married with a young son, Forester had originally been a tailor by trade. Being very religious, he felt he had been called to devote himself to a more suitable vocation. In 1853 he had joined a training institution at Bedford, with the intention that afterwards he would work as a home missionary.

Mrs Saltmarsh believed that he was just the kind of man she required, and in May 1855 she engaged him to visit the poor in their cottages around the area, where he would read and talk about the scriptures to them, and preach at a chapel in the neighbourhood every Sunday. For the next twelve months he carried out his duties conscientiously and with great enthusiasm. Very earnest and active, he achieved plenty of respect for his labours. Nevertheless, Mrs Saltmarsh, and other people with whom he came into contact, found him rather eccentric, and she thought his intellectual abilities were not quite suited for the work.

In the summer of 1856 she warned Charles that she was giving him three months' notice to find alternative employment. As he had a wife and child to support, she was prepared to help the family. With some financial assistance, she helped the disappointed Mrs Forester to open a grocery shop in Embrook. When the situation became common knowledge, there was a good deal of sympathy and goodwill in the neighbourhood. For all his faults, Mr Forester was much liked, and evidently to be pitied as well. Mrs Forester was much admired for her fortitude in this trying business, and perhaps partly because of this the shop was a great success.

While he worked out the remaining weeks of his notice, Mr Forester's physical and mental health began to deteriorate, and it was thought that he was probably in the early stages of consumption. As soon as his missionary duties were completed, he was sent as an in-patient to Brompton Hospital in Middlesex. He was discharged in October, apparently better, but instead of contacting his wife he took lodgings in York Terrace, Stepney. While he was there his conduct became increasingly peculiar and his neighbours demanded that he be removed. By 10 November he had returned home to Embrook.

His wife and neighbours found him very depressed and in urgent need of medical care. They made arrangements for him to spend some time in a convalescent home in Bournemouth, and on 12 November he was accompanied to the railway station by Mr Sparkes, his successor as Mrs Saltmarsh's home missionary. While they were waiting for the train to arrive, Mr Sparkes thought his charge so enfeebled that he brought him straight home again pending further arrangements. The next day he seemed very lethargic and unwell, but that night he slept much better.

The following morning, 14 November, Mrs Forester got up, leaving her husband and their five-year-old son Samuel in bed together. Her husband came downstairs about an hour later, while she was serving in the shop, and she thought he was going out into the garden. He was away longer than she expected him to be, and as there was no sound from upstairs she thought it strange that Samuel should not have woken up and come downstairs.

Nothing could have prepared her for the horror which met her gaze when she went upstairs to check on her son. Samuel's lifeless body lay on the bed, his throat cut and head almost severed from his body, with blood covering the pillow and sheets. She raised the alarm, and her neighbours tried to find her husband, but in vain. He had walked into town to look for a policeman. At 8.45 a.m. he knocked on the door of Sergeant John Bostock of the Berkshire County Police. The sergeant was still in bed, but got up, opened the bedroom window, and asked Mr Forester what he wanted.

'I have come to give myself in charge for murdering my little boy,' was the reply. The policeman came downstairs and took him to the station, where he made a statement. When asked his name, he said, 'Forester'. Asked where his little boy was, he said he did not know, and had forgotten. As to where he lived, he pointed in the direction of his house. Bostock handcuffed him, and saw that Forester's hands were covered in blood. Together they went to the Foresters' cottage, where the still-warm body of Samuel lay on the bed. The blood on the bedclothes had not yet congealed.

At Wokingham police station, Mr Forester was 'in a state of some excitement'. Sweat was pouring down his face, he seemed very confused, and the sergeant thought him barely conscious of what he was saying. Letters were found on him, one addressed to his brother, alluding to his own death and his fears as to who would take care of Samuel if anything happened to him. He may have been considering suicide.

That afternoon, Forester appeared before Mr Fitzgerald, the county magistrate. Two neighbours and a surgeon joined the police in giving evidence. The first was Mary Evans, who lived with her husband James two doors down from the Foresters at Embrook and knew the family well. She said that Mr Forester had always seemed very fond of his wife and son. After another neighbour had raised the alarm, she went to the house and found Mrs Forester in a very distressed condition, saying that he had killed the boy. After going upstairs to see the dead child, she came down and sat with Mrs Forester until the arrival of Sergeant Bostock.

After the policeman had told the hearing about his involvement, Mary Langley, another neighbour, took the stand. That morning she had seen Mr Forester walk past her house on his way into Wokingham, and heard the terrible news about twenty minutes later. She went to see Mrs Forester and found her sitting in the front room, 'in a very excited state'. Going upstairs, she saw the child's body, and stayed in the house

Market Place, Wokingham, c. 1900.

until the arrival of Mr Weight, the surgeon. They then went upstairs together, and she carefully lifted the boy's body, to reveal a bloodstained razor.

Mr Weight said he had examined the body of the deceased child, and found an incised wound across the throat, dividing the trachea, oesophagus and principal blood vessels, and vertebral column. The head was almost severed, and the wound was quite warm. At this point Constable Davis produced the razor, which he said had been given to him by Mrs Langley.

The last witness to be called was Superintendent Crook of the Berkshire Police. That morning he had had custody of Mr Forester. During that time the prisoner had said, more than once, 'Oh dear! Oh dear! I wouldn't mind giving anything to undo what I have done. I loved my little boy, and no one loved him better than I did. I can't think what I did it for, I'm sure.'

A reporter noticed that Mr Fitzgerald did not ask the witnesses any questions during the hearing. Described somewhat oddly as 'rather an intelligent man, apparently very respectable, [with] large mournful eyes,' the magistrate 'appeared almost careless as to what was going on, but evidently was in a state of great mental and bodily depression.' Forester was committed to the county gaol. An inquest was held under Rupert Clark, the county coroner, on the following afternoon, and a verdict of 'wilful murder' was returned.

Forester went on trial at Oxford Assizes on 3 March 1857, but it was little more than a formality. After Mr Skinner had given evidence for the prosecution, Mr Huddleston for the defence said that the prisoner was obviously deprived of his reason when he committed the murder, and it had been shown beyond doubt that for years his conduct had been very eccentric. If he was not insane, he was perilously close to it; he had suffered from severe depression for a long time, and it was beyond dispute that he had been very fond of his son. Further testimony was given by two gentlemen from the Town Missions Society at Taunton, who said they had engaged the prisoner as a scripture reader two years previously, and even then he 'showed such strangeness of conduct' that they could not continue to employ him.

In summing up, the judge said that the murder was clearly committed at a moment when the prisoner was deprived of his reason. He directed the jury to find him not guilty, and sentenced him to custody at Her Majesty's pleasure.

7

'I DON'T KNOW WHAT I'M ABOUT'

Windsor, 1862

John and Anne Gould lived at Clarence Clump, Clewer Lane, near Windsor. Anne had a thirteen-year-old daughter, Elizabeth, from a previous marriage, who lodged nearby with the family for whom she worked as a domestic servant. The couple also had a younger daughter, Hannah, aged seven. A powerfully built man, John had at first lived at Windsor when he was apprenticed to a trunk-maker, but he was dismissed for being unreliable. As he had no skills to speak of, he became a general labourer, and since moving to Clewer in about 1856 he had worked as a bricklayer's labourer. Having been employed at some time by most of the local builders, he was well known in the area, not only for his trade, but also for his quarrelsome and sometimes violent behaviour. Thirty-nine years old in 1861, he was well known to the police as a man who would not hesitate to use his fists if he was cornered, and he had already served three terms of imprisonment for violence. His fourth major brush with the law was to be for a much more serious offence.

On the morning of 30 December 1861, Mrs Gould went to work as usual at Windsor Dispensary and Infirmary, where she worked as a day nurse. Her husband was not working at the time, as there was not much call for labourers at that time of year. However, he had enough money put aside to spend the morning drinking in his local, the Prince of Wales. He and his wife had left Hannah in the care of Sarah Clark, the wife of a police sergeant, and a friend who lived about five doors away. There were several children for Hannah to play with, including Mrs Clark's two children, nine-year-old Harriet and five-year-old Daniel, and six-year-old Tommy Webb, the son of another neighbour in the road.

Early that afternoon, Hannah returned home so that she could get a fire going in the parlour, to make it warm for when her parents returned, and heat some potatoes for her father's dinner. As she had had ample experience of his uncertain temper, and had often had her ears boxed when he was not satisfied with her behaviour, she wanted to give him as little cause for complaint as possible. The other children decided they would follow her and give her a hand to help light the fire and tidy the house.

It was mid-afternoon when they heard heavy footsteps approach, and saw the door open as Mr Gould reappeared. Hannah only needed to glance at his face to see that he had had too much to drink as usual and would probably be in a bad mood. He shouted at the other children to get out and close the door after them. Harriet, the eldest, stood in the doorway, but the younger ones trooped out. Turning to Hannah, he told her angrily, 'You're a naughty little girl not to clean up the place.'

'I could not do it,' she answered apologetically. Sensing that there might be trouble ahead, Harriet asked her to come away, but Gould snapped, 'No, I want to do something with her.' Reluctantly, Harriet left and ran back to her house, ready to tell her mother what had happened.

Hannah moved away from her father in terror, but she was not quick enough as he grabbed a razor from a shelf, picked her up and cut her throat. At the sight of the heavily bleeding wound, he briefly came to his senses and impulsively went round to Mrs Clark's house, calling out loudly, 'Mrs Clark, I want you.' Like Harriet, she knew too well of the ill-treatment Hannah had suffered at the hands of her drunken father. With trepidation, she followed him back to his house. When they entered the house she saw a large quantity of blood on the floor, and then noticed Hannah lying at the bottom of the stairs on her knees, her head lying on the bottom step, blood pouring from her throat as she feebly tried to speak, yet with no words coming out. Gould was still holding the bloodstained razor.

'Oh! You vagabond!' she exclaimed. 'You've cut the child's throat.'

'I done it, I done it,' he answered. Mrs Clark ran from the house, screaming, 'Murder! Murder!' and determined to protect her own children, just in case he was about to go on the rampage in the street.

Other neighbours had come outside to see what the noise was. Some of them were in time to watch Gould drag Hannah outside, swearing at her that he would die for her as he flung her against the wall. Samuel Wilkins, a boy who lived next door to the Goulds, ran towards Hannah, still breathing feebly, and picked her up. Two other neighbours went to alert the police and another labourer in the street, Charles Coker, took Hannah from Samuel's arms, carrying her as fast as he could to the Windsor Infirmary, about a quarter of a mile away. She was still alive when they started their journey, and she tried feebly to speak to him, but the words would not come out. But by the time they reached the infirmary, she was dead. The surgeon, James Ellison, examined the body and found a five-inch wound across her throat, which had cut through the jugular vein.

Meanwhile, Constable Peter Radbourne had arrived to arrest Gould. It took the work of two or three burly neighbours to help overpower him as he put up a struggle, but at length they took him to the police station at Windsor. As they went, Gould told them that he had 'done it' because he was tired of his life, and he was happy now that he had done so.

On 31 December he was taken before the Mayor, W.B. Holderness, for the case to be heard in the justice rooms at Windsor Guildhall. Hannah's inquest was due to take place simultaneously in the council chamber, thus allowing witnesses to move from one to the other. Constable Radbourne said that when he arrested the prisoner he appeared the worse for drink, but was not actually drunk. When asked why he had killed his daughter, Gould said that he came home to get some dinner, she had started crying and it annoyed him. He added that he was very sorry for what he had done. Meanwhile, the inquest heard similar evidence from other witnesses, and established that Hannah Gould had died while Coker was carrying her to the infirmary. It was pointed out that if Gould had summoned medical help after attacking her, instead of throwing her outside against the wall, her life might have been saved. The surgeon had confirmed that hers was the body of a healthy child, and that the cause of death had been the severed vein in her throat. A verdict of wilful murder was returned.

The hearing before the Mayor was adjourned until New Year's Day, and a new witness was brought forward. Reuben Turner, a carpenter who lived in Clewer Lane, had been drinking with Gould in the Prince of Wales on the day of the murder. During their conversation, said Turner, Gould mentioned that he was going to be locked up the following day. When asked why, he replied, 'for murder', adding that he would no longer be alive on 1 April. Turner endured a few more minutes of these maudlin drunken ramblings before leaving the pub. It now looked as if Gould had intended to kill somebody in cold blood, though whether he had decided it would be his own daughter or some unfortunate random victim in the street where he lived, nobody could say.

Gould was then asked to speak. All he could say in mitigation was that it would never have happened if he had not been drinking. As soon as he had anything to drink, 'I don't know what I'm about.' He was committed by the Mayor for trial on a charge of wilful murder at the next Reading Assizes, and escorted by Sergeant Noble through hissing crowds to Windsor and Eton railway station, from where he travelled in a closed compartment to Reading. As the gaol came into view, he commented to Noble that they were looking at what would be his last home in the world. He was remanded in custody for the next two months until the start of the trial, which opened on 28 February 1862 under Judge Baron Channell.

The court at Reading opened that day at 9 a.m. to enormous crowds and packed galleries. It did not escape the attention of the press that there were many 'persons of genteel appearance' and 'a considerable sprinkle of females'. As he stood in the dock and was asked how he would plead to the charge of wilfully murdering his daughter, Gould answered 'guilty'. There were several witnesses for the prosecution and none for the defence, so the undersheriff had instructed a local lawyer, George Russell, to defend the prisoner.

For the prosecution J.O. Griffiths, began his case by reminding the jury that Mr Gould stood charged with the most serious crime known to the laws of the country, and proceeded to question the witnesses, who between them recounted everything they had seen on that tragic afternoon.

Russell also questioned the witnesses with great care, quick to seize on any statements or suggestions that there might have been something peculiar about the prisoner's personality during the weeks prior to the murder. It was possible that he was suicidal, or that his sanity could be called into question. When he addressed the jury, he drew attention to Gould's suicide attempts some years previously, and the fact that he had been involved in a brawl which left him with a severe head wound which might help to explain, if not excuse, his actions. When one witness said he had called out to Gould while returning to his house and thought he looked sullen, Russell asked whether this was a man intent on murder, or suffering from temporary insanity. Was he 'of sound memory and discretion at the time he committed the act?' Drunkenness was no excuse, but insanity was. He suggested that Mrs Gould, who was prevented by law from speaking in her husband's defence, might possibly hold the key to his behaviour on the day in question.

Despite Russell's eloquent defence and a plea for mercy, the jury were unmoved. It took them just ten minutes to reach a unanimous verdict, which then had to wait

Windsor railway station.

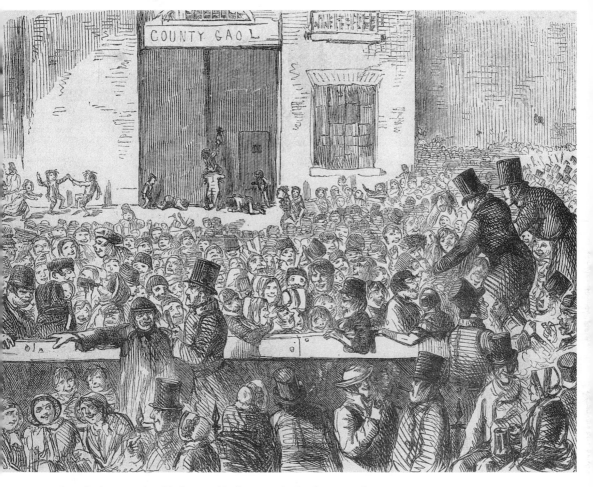

Outside the county gaol before a public hanging, 1849, from Punch.

until a charge of robbery against another prisoner was brought in the same court. The foreman then announced a verdict of guilty. Gould showed no emotion as Judge Channell sentenced him to death, though sobs were heard from the gallery. He left the dock after saying a few words to the deputy governor of the gaol.

On the Monday before his execution, he was visited by his sister, who was so shaken that she fainted shortly after entering his cell. On the following day, Mrs Gould and her daughter Elizabeth came to say their tearful farewell. His wife had forgiven him, and the couple prayed together. He had already resigned himself to his coming fate, and for much of the night before his execution he prayed, being joined in prayer next morning by the chaplain, the Revd J.B. Colville.

Gould was almost certainly unaware that strenuous efforts were being made to appeal against the verdict. A number of Berkshire gentlemen, including the Mayor

William Calcraft, executioner from 1829 until his retirement in 1874.

of Reading, travelled to London on 13 March in order to seek an audience with the Home Secretary, Sir George Grey. They claimed they were seeking mercy for a man whose crime fell outside the definition of murder. Nevertheless, Grey told them that the law had to take its course.

The execution was scheduled for 14 March. At 1 a.m. on that day Gould rose from his bed and knelt down in prayer for several minutes, then lay down again. He awoke about three hours later, and spent the next few hours in religious exercises with the chaplain. At some point, he asked to be allowed to give his fellow prisoners some words of advice:

> My last dying words to my fellow prisoners are that they will all take warning from me – that they will abstain from drunkenness. Drink has been the ruin both of my body and my soul. It has robbed my conscience, so that I had not the fear of God before my eyes. I hope that they will pray earnestly to God to keep them from temptation, and that they will live nearer to God than I have hitherto done until now.

The governor, Mr Ferry, and undersheriff, Mr Blandy, went to the cell to call Gould shortly before midday on 14 March. At the time Gould was deep in prayer. He thanked the chaplain for all he had done, and asked him to return the Bible, which his stepdaughter had lent to him, after his death. He then said, 'May the Lord bless you, and I hope He will give you many blessings for what you have done for me. Give my love to my people, and tell them I remember them.'

Gould was executed by hangman William Calcraft. The local newspaper reported that there was a vast crowd of people from all walks of society present. Despite the grim nature of the spectacle, even mothers with small children in their arms were among the thousands who had come to watch. It was literally their last opportunity, for Gould was the last man to die in public on the gallows in Berkshire. Six years later, legislation was passed to ensure that all convicted murderers would in future be hanged in private.

8

DEATH OF THE COOK FAMILY

Windsor, 1864

In 1853 Mary Ann Pope married John Richard Cook in Eton. She was a laundress, while he was a barber employed by Eton College, supplementing his income by working from their home at Old Windsor, and together the couple had five daughters. John, aged about forty, had at some stage taken to the bottle, inevitably losing much of his custom as a result and with it his financial security. He ran up large debts and eventually filed for bankruptcy. Although he managed to get by with some money from the college and various local benefactors, it was still a struggle to make ends meet.

Mary evidently provided her husband with a purpose in life; when she died in childbirth in July 1864, he more or less gave up working and became something of a recluse. Only rarely would he speak to his neighbours or other members of the family. The children always looked well-nourished as all the money the family received was controlled by the local vicar, the Revd John Blunt, who tried to ensure that it was spent on food and not alcohol.

Neighbours took it upon themselves to keep a watchful eye on the motherless girls. On Sunday 2 October 1864, they were concerned that nobody had seen either John or his daughters all weekend. They alerted Constable George Lovell of the Berkshire Constabulary, and at about 2 p.m. on Sunday afternoon he came round to the cottage. He looked through the windows and saw children lying on a mattress on the floor. As there was no answer at the door, he broke a window and entered the front room. The first thing he saw was a pail containing about half a gallon of blood. Looking around further, he saw a razor, covered with blood and hairs, on the mantelpiece. In the front room he was greeted by the pitiful sight of three children lying side by side on the mattress. Five-year-old Agnes Josephine, four-year-old Eugenie, and two-year-old Louisa Elizabeth were all dead. Preparing himself for further horrors Lovell went upstairs, where he found the eldest child, nine-year-old Mary Ann, in a bedroom, lying on the bed with a wound across her throat. She was still breathing, but had 'something black about her mouth'. In the next room, lying on another bed, was her father, also alive but with a deep cut across his throat. Next to him was six-year-old Adelaide, who had a bandage around her neck. The constable assumed that she had a similar wound.

Next he found three bottles, which he thought had contained poison. Cook saw him, and gasped weakly, 'For God's sake, give me some water, Lovell, I am famishing with thirst!' He appeared in great agony.

Lovell immediately sent for his colleague Inspector Reece, and the surgeon, Dr Pearl, who both arrived at about the same time. They found Cook lying in bed, vomiting black fluid. When Reece questioned him, he said nothing about the children, but admitted he had poisoned himself. Reece had a look through a chest of drawers and found a half-pint bottle about half full with vitriol, or sulphuric acid. In another room he found a basin containing tea, which had been poisoned. Probing further, he persuaded Cook to admit that he had taken poison, and he added that Mary Ann had given some of the tea to the other children. When asked if he had told her to do so, he refused to answer.

After inspecting the bloodstained razor, and seeing the pail of blood, the officers decided that Cook must have cut his throat downstairs and then gone up to his bed to die. They also thought that he had dressed the wound on Adelaide's throat, as it was clean and free from blood. Later still they found her clothes, saturated with blood. The two doctors, Pearl and Gooch, sewed up the wounds in her throat, and Reece then took her and Mary Ann in a cab to the Windsor Infirmary. As for Cook, the blood had congealed around the wound to his throat. Despite medical attention, he was beyond saving, and died at about 7 p.m.

When the cottage was searched more thoroughly, the officers found several letters underneath his pillow, addressed to various people. They all clearly stated his intention to poison his children, and then destroy himself, requested that no post-mortem examination should be held on any of them, and stipulated that the burials should not take place at the parish's expense.

Nevertheless, the due processes of the law had to take place. After the post-mortem, an inquest was held on 5 October at the boardroom of the workhouse in Old Windsor, under the coroner Rupert Clarke. Joseph Brant, a gardener and Cook's brother-in-law, referred to the death of Mrs Cook about three months previously, and said he had seen Cook and his family about three or four times a week. On Monday 26 September they had had a drink together at the Wheatsheaf Inn, but apparently no words passed between them.

'I had not had any conversation with Cook since his wife's death,' said Brant. 'He seemed to have very little to say to me. I had not noticed any alteration in him since the death of his wife.' He also said that the deceased had had little if any employment since becoming a widower, was bankrupt while he was living at Slough, and had been supported by his wife up to the time of her death. Brant also added that he could give no information as to why the deaths should have taken place, though it must have appeared evident that, with the burden of supporting the family and with his inability or unwillingness to find work, he saw no other way out. He also remarked, in somewhat contradictory fashion, that his brother-in-law 'was a high-spirited man and reserved in his manner.'

Next to give evidence was Brant's wife, Caroline, who was also Mrs Cook's sister. She had not seen the Cook family very often, and she thought John and his children must have been heavily dependent on the kindness of the neighbouring gentry since his wife's death. Caroline's final conversation with him had been about three or four weeks before his death. She last met him at Windsor, when he told her that the children were well. She saw the eldest girl more frequently than the others, the last time having been on the evening of Friday 30 September at about 6.30 p.m. She said that her father had sent her to borrow two candles, and Caroline lent her one. The girl added that her sisters were not very well. Caroline did not notice anything particular in her manner or appearance.

She saw Adelaide at about 4.15 on Sunday afternoon, upstairs in a back bedroom. They had no conversation, and the girl seemed too ill to speak. In conclusion, Caroline said she did not know any relative who could give any information about Cook's proceedings during the final week. Adelaide had said nothing to her on Friday evening about her father being unkind to her, and she had not noticed any change in his habits since his wife died.

At this point, one of the jurymen said he had recently seen Adelaide Cook sporting a black eye. The vicar added that she had no such disfigurement when she went to see him on the Friday. He also made a statement saying that Cook had applied to him in September to write out a petition for him, which he declined to do. He did, however, write a letter which Cook took to several gentlemen in the neighbourhood, which helped him to obtain a few more pounds. £2 5s was received by the clergy in addition to what was given directly to Cook. From that money he had received weekly supplies of grocery and other necessities, and these continued right up to the time he killed himself.

Mrs Arnold, who had lived near Cook, said she saw him on Saturday at about 1 p.m. She had not spoken to him for a couple of months, and they only exchanged a few words. About a week before that she had chatted with Mary Ann, and the last time she saw Adelaide was on the Saturday, between 11 a.m. and noon, when Cook was playing with her and Mary Ann in the garden. The others girls she had last seen on Thursday.

Cook, she went on, had been a disagreeable neighbour, and resented people looking in on the children when he was at home. While he seemed kind enough to them – an opinion borne out by subsequent witnesses – he never wanted anybody else to set foot inside his house. In spite of rumours in the area, Mrs Arnold had never seen him drink. It had been part of his normal routine to visit Eton College and cut the boys' hair every Saturday, but only a few people used to come to his house to have their hair cut, these being the only people he was prepared to allow beyond his front door. He had told her that he received 6s a week, paid quarterly, and also received a quantity of bread, usually four 2lb loaves, from the college every Saturday. On the last Saturday he was alive, between 1 and 2 p.m., he was walking up and down his garden with his arms folded, and 'a very wild look in his eyes'. She was sure that if he had been carrying anything in his hand at the time, he would not have hesitated to try and kill her. When he saw her he walked towards her as if he was going to tell her something, but his appearance completely unnerved her and she went straight back into her house for safety.

The children had never complained to her for want of food, and they generally looked well fed, though she did not know whether there was any person who attended to the children. She did not hear them make any noise on the Friday or Saturday, and after Saturday night she saw nothing of them, or of their father.

Henry Pope, a gardener, was also a brother-in-law of Cook, and lived a quarter of a mile away from him. He said that he had seen Cook 'in liquor, but only occasionally'. When Mary Ann came to see him on Friday 30 September to borrow 2s, he invited her to come and have a little drink of beer with him, as he was having his dinner. She declined; as she had had a glass of ale at home in the morning and it had made her quite sick. He had not noticed any difference in her appearance, and after leaving him she went and played with some other children nearby. That evening at about 7 p.m. he saw her and Adelaide playing with their father, who asked him if he could borrow 6d.

When questioned by the jury, Pope said that Cook had 'appeared very strange at the time of his wife's death, and did not appear willing to have a woman to sit up with her.'

Brant then took the stand again to say that Cook seemed to him 'a desperate kind of man'. When his wife died there were strange reports 'tending to the defamation of his character,' but he could not tell whether there was any substance to them, or if they were just wild rumour.

Constable Lovell, who said that he had known Cook and his family well and seen them regularly, described his entry into the premises, the discovery of the bodies, and his summoning of Dr Pearl and Inspector Reece. The latter said that he saw several bottles, which were thought to contain laudanum, and in a basin at the foot of the bed on which Mary Ann was lying, some tea containing vitriol. He asked Adelaide if that was the tea her father gave her, and she said it was. Then he asked her when her father gave it to her, and she said 'on Friday', at about dinnertime. Although she spoke in a very low voice, she was quite conscious. He then searched a cupboard in the room where Cook was lying and found some children's clothes, all saturated with blood. Downstairs, in the front room, he found two memorials or petitions addressed to the nobility and gentry of Old Windsor, in which Cook appealed to them for assistance. He also found a letter written by the vicar, stating that he was prepared to receive subscriptions for Cook; an agreement between Mr Clarke, the lessee of Windsor Theatre, and Cook, who had agreed to pay £10 for the proceeds of a night's performance; a summons for £3 18s 6d, disposed of at the April court; two bills from Mr Tussell, a Slough tradesman; and an order of bankruptcy dated 1862. Much of this evidence was corroborated by Inspector Reece.

Constable Hailey from the Berkshire Constabulary, stationed at Clewer, testified to having found some letters from Cook under his pillow, one addressed to his brother, and the other to the vicar. There were several other papers, each written in pencil. The vicar then read Cook's letter to him, which stated that the spirit of his dead wife used to visit him every night, imploring him to come to her and bring the children with him, 'before the place at his side was taken by someone else'. Had she believed, or feared, that her husband might have taken a mistress or a second wife? The letters also apparently told him that she believed the vicar, the Revd Blunt, would allow him and the children to be buried by her side.

The other papers, read by Inspector Reece, contained Cook's request for his brother to see to the funeral of himself and the children, and a plea that Mr Pearl 'would not cut and hack their bodies about after death, as he could see the cause.' In one he stated that he had almost lost his senses. This would never have happened had his wife still been alive, as he loved her so dearly, that they loved the children, and that he had prayed to God to forgive him his sins. The vicar identified the handwriting as that of Cook.

Mr Pearl, the Windsor surgeon, said that he had known Cook and attended his wife about four months previously. He had last seen Cook at about 4 p.m. on Sunday afternoon, when he was lying in bed looking very pale. His beard was clotted with blood, which also covered his right shoulder and arm. He saw his throat was cut, but the blood had congealed and the beard partly covered it, so that he could not see the extent of the wound. When the surgeon questioned him he admitted that he had taken vitriol, was constantly vomiting dark black acid matter, and complaining of considerable pain, begging for something to drink. Pearl administered some remedies, which he thought might help, and then went to the infirmary with the two eldest girls.

On returning to the cottage at about 5.30 p.m., he found Cook worse, and asked him where he had cut his throat. Cook told the surgeon that he had done it the previous night, downstairs, and that they had been bleeding and in pain all night. Pearl then asked him when he had given the children poison, but he denied having given them any poison at all, saying that it was the eldest child who had administered it to them. Pearl said he supposed it was at Cook's direction, and received no reply, but Cook said that when he cut the second child's throat he thought he had worked himself up to a pitch of madness.

Cook's condition gradually worsened and he died at about 7 p.m. In his last hours he appeared perfectly calm, and answered every question in a rational manner.

In conducting the post-mortem, Pearl established what had already been apparent – that Cook had died from the effect of corrosive poison, which, however, 'did not interfere with his intellect even at the last moments of his life.' He also performed an examination on the body of Agnes Josephine. The front of the body was quite green and beginning to decompose rapidly. There were vivid marks over the rest of the body, which were post-mortem changes. He examined all the organs of both cavities separately, and found no morbid appearance in any of them. When he opened the head, he found the vessels of the membranes of the brain full of dark fluid blood. The brain itself was in a healthy state, not congested, there was no effusion in any of its cavities, and the stomach contained some undigested food. There was no odour of poison of any kind in the stomach, but as he found no natural cause to account for death, given the circumstances he was sure that the child had died from the effects of poison.

The bottle produced by Inspector Reece smelt of opium, and he thought the youngest children had been dead by Friday. The bodies were well nourished, and there was an abundance of fat in each body.

Lovell was briefly recalled to the witness box. He said he had found two loaves and other provisions in the house. The family had not been starving, and Cook had no reason to fear that they would starve.

In conclusion the coroner briefly addressed the jury. They were out for about fifteen minutes, before returning a verdict that Cook 'destroyed himself and his children by poison, but that there was no satisfactory evidence to show the state of his mind at the time.'

St Andrew's Church, Clewer.

Mary Ann died from the effects of the poison at about 12.30 a.m. on 5 October. Alone among the family Adelaide survived, and the 1871 census returns revealed that she was then living at the Female Orphan Asylum in Beddington, Surrey. Ten years later she had returned to Old Windsor, where she lived with her uncle, John Arthur.

On 7 October, the dead children were all laid to rest in a single grave, close to their mother, at St Andrew's Church, Clewer. Despite what he claimed his dead wife had wished, their father's body was buried without ceremony in the farthest corner of the churchyard.

9

FOUND DROWNED

Reading, 1864

On 1 August 1864 Emma Legge, her husband James, an upholsterer, and their three children, five-year-old Flora, three-year-old Louis, and Napoleon, a baby of three months, arrived at Reading from Tunbridge Wells by train. Having found lodgings for them all at the Rising Sun Inn, Forbury, James left them that evening to sleep at the Spread Eagle in another part of town. Emma had the children, a small sum of money, and a few pieces of furniture. She stayed at the Rising Sun for a few days, then went to an inn in Minster Street until 8 August, selling the remaining furniture for £2. After paying for her lodgings she settled a few small bills, leaving her with about 3s. On the evening of 9 August she found room for herself and the children at the Jack of Newbury in Bridge Street, where they spent the night.

The next day she was up soon after 6 a.m. to dress herself and the family. Just before 7 a.m. she went to William Boseley, a furniture dealer in Horn Street, to hire a perambulator so she could take the children out. It looked as if it was about to rain, and Mr Boseley said he thought it would be too cold to take them out so early, but she was determined to go. He let her borrow the perambulator, watched her put the children into it and walk along Caversham Road, and turn down into a yard adjoining the White Hart Inn, towards the Thames towpath.

A little later William Jacobs, working in a garden on the opposite side of the river, noticed the empty perambulator. Looking around to see anybody nearby who might be in charge, he saw what looked like a human body floating on the surface of the river. He got into his employer's pleasure boat, pulled across the river, and within a few yards of the bank he saw three children and a woman within a short distance of each other, all dead. They were taken to an outhouse belonging to the White Hart Inn. The children were already very cold, though the woman was still warm, and under Mr F.A. Bulley, the surgeon, attempts were made to revive her, but in vain.

That afternoon, Mr Blandy, the borough coroner, held an inquest in the White Hart. Mr Bulley said that at 9.30 that morning he had been called to the inn to attend to the bodies, which had just been pulled out of the water just above the bridge. He found them lying in a stable adjoining the inn, with several persons trying to resuscitate them. Judging by the temperature of the mother's body when he first saw her, he estimated that the children had been in the water for between half an hour and an hour before being taken out of the water. There were no signs of violence on any of the bodies.

Mr Jacobs then described how he had found them. He said he took them out of the water, placed them in the boat, and asked his ten-year-old son to go and fetch his friend Mr Piper to come and help, as someone had drowned. After lifting the woman up by the head and holding her up, Piper and another friend arrived in a punt and helped her out. The perambulator was about 4ft from the edge of the water, which was about 12ft deep, where the bodies were found. The two younger children were floating on their backs, while the eldest and the woman were both lying face downwards in the water. They had all been immersed, and on rising were kept up by their clothes, with their hats in the water. In the perambulator was a purse containing only three halfpence, two paper bags containing broken biscuits, and another halfpenny at the bottom. The two elder children had been eating biscuits, and as there was milk coming from his mouth, the youngest must have suckled from his mother shortly before being thrown into the water.

Emma Legge's brother, James King, who lived at Whitley, said he had seen his sister at about 10.30 a.m. on Saturday 6 August. The last time he saw the three children alive was later that same day. While he did not know her husband, he met a man in the street whom he supposed from a description given to him to be James Legge. On speaking to him, he found it was a different man altogether. He was not sure whether his sister had actually been married to Legge, though she told him she was, and he had no reason to believe that she was not telling the truth. One day that week she had given him the address of her husband's brother at Tunbridge

Wells, and she asked him to write to her brother-in-law to find out if her husband had gone back there to work, but he received no answer.

The River Thames, below Caversham Lock. (© Dr Neil Clifton)

James King had spent about seventeen years in Australia, returning on 19 June that year. Since then he had seen his sister four or five times. She came to Reading on 1 August, and he confirmed that she had had lodgings taken for her by her husband, though he himself did not stay long. She told him her husband had gone away drinking, she was very short of money, did not know what he was going to do about work, and expected him back at any hour. He asked her if she would go and live with him if he got work in Reading, and he said he would try and support her and the children. She said she would not, as she had no desire to 'be under obligation to anyone', then talked of selling the things she had with her, and of returning to Tunbridge Wells to try and find her husband.

When the coroner asked him why he thought his sister had come to Reading, he said he thought she had come to live there. He also thought her husband had sent a large amount of goods and luggage by rail, and the children were following, so she expected they would be setting up home there. When the coroner asked whether she had seemed 'in a despondent state', he said his sister appeared very low-spirited because of her husband's absence and drinking, and she was sure he had gone back to Tunbridge Wells. The coroner said that was all the evidence he was prepared to lay before the jury at that stage, but as it was desirable to find the husband if possible, an adjournment had to take place. Meanwhile, Superintendent Peck would contact the police at Tunbridge Wells to find out if he was there, and in the hope of finding any more evidence which might enable them to arrive at a verdict.

The inquest was resumed on 15 August at the Public Office, Reading. Mr J. Cave Paine, a solicitor from Frimley, informed Mr Blandy that he had come to watch proceedings on behalf of the man he called 'the alleged husband of the deceased woman'.

By now several more witnesses, including members of the family, were able to provide a more detailed picture of events of the preceding few days. The first was Mrs Ruffell, landlady of the Berkshire Hog, where Emma Legge had taken lodgings for a while. Mrs Ruffell stated that on arrival Emma had brought with her a mattress, eight chairs, blankets and several other articles of furniture and bedding, which she wanted to sell as she was sure her husband had returned to Tunbridge Wells. When he left, she said, he had 25 sovereigns in a leather bag, four sovereigns in one pocket, and 10s in another. Mrs Ruffell said Emma often talked about her husband, and did not seem unduly distressed, though 'she looked wild about the eyes'. He had previously left her, she said, but he always returned and told her where he had spent every night, and she had always found that he was telling the truth.

Mrs Legge kept to her room, and often said, 'I've given all up'. She spoke very little to the children, and allowed them to remain undressed for hours in the morning before dressing them. Mrs Ruffell thought that they were being neglected. She begged Mrs Legge to get food for them, and gave her money for the purpose. Mrs Legge kept on saying how little money she had, and Mrs Ruffell suggested she should get a broker to value the goods. If she did so and if the broker said they were worth £4, she would give her £4 10s. Mrs Ruffell added that a Margaret Coles of Whitley came to offer her 15s for the goods, and an argument ensued.

Mrs Coles, the next witness to speak, said she had known Emma Legge for about twenty years, and thought she had been married for about six or seven years. She had last seen Emma on 4 August, when she went to her brother's house, saying her husband had left her and she could not find him. Seeing her again on 8 August at Mrs Ruffell's, she asked if Emma had had any more success. Emma said she had not, and doubted if she would ever see her husband again. Her only plans were to try and find the money to pay Mrs Ruffell, take her goods away and go to Kent. From the way her husband had treated her lately, he would probably never return, and for the last five weeks he had been continually with his brother and his wife, leaving after breakfast and not returning until about 11 p.m. She wanted to go into Kent and see whether her father-in-law and brother-in-law were there or had gone with her husband.

As Mrs Coles was about to leave, Emma asked her to call again in the morning. She did so, to find Emma with the baby on her lap. She saw the furniture and goods had been moved around, and asked whether the broker had been. Emma said he had not, and that Mrs Ruffell wanted to buy the goods, but she was short of money, and in any case she would not let Mrs Ruffell have the things as she had been 'telling people below about her', and about her husband leaving her. She wanted to clear her things out of the room the same day. When Mrs Coles asked her how much she wanted for the goods, the answer was, 'Margaret, you can have them if you can get money to pay Mrs Ruffell,' but she would not touch anything without her setting a price on them. Emma repeated that if she could find money to pay Mrs Ruffell, and also take her and the children into Kent, the goods were hers. Mrs Coles gave her 17s 6d, saying it was all she had but she could get more later. Emma then paid Mrs Ruffell 13s. Mrs Coles then went to George Smith in Mill Lane and borrowed a sovereign which she took to Mrs Legge, who told her she 'did not want all this; 10s would have been enough.' She told Emma she would need the rest when she went to Kent, but Emma said she would be all right.

Mrs Ruffell then came into the room and offered Emma £1 for a mattress, but Emma said it was already sold. Mrs Ruffell told Mrs Coles she would not have the goods for more than a couple of days before somebody came and took them away, and told Emma that if she heard of her husband and gave her the same amount of money, she should have them again. Mrs Ruffell said she would write to the Police Superintendent at Tunbridge Wells to ask if they had come away from there in debt, so they would know where to find Mrs Legge, who with her husband 'had been going about the country cheating people'. The increasingly heated exchange ended with Mrs Ruffell threatening to turn the Legges out into the street, and Mrs Coles telling her she could fetch a policeman if she wanted to.

Asked if there had been any dispute with Mrs Ruffell, Mrs Coles denied it. She told Mrs Ruffell to fetch a policeman, and if she was doing anything wrong she would find out when he came. A van came and collected the goods.

The next witness called was Thomas Atto, of the Rising Sun, Forbury. He said that on 1 August Mr and Mrs Legge and the children had come to his inn and asked for lodgings. Although he was unable to offer them all accommodation, he agreed to let the mother and children stay there while Mr Legge went to seek rooms elsewhere. He soon returned to say he had found another place, and then Atto heard them arguing. Mr Legge then left, apparently to continue his search, but he did not return that night and the wife and children had to stay there. When he returned the following morning, she upbraided him for leaving her and the children alone in a strange place. He gave the impression of being devoted to the family, and when she took him to task he 'did not appear at all quarrelsome'.

Several other witnesses were called. The most significant was James Legge's brother John, who said at the start of his evidence that though his brother and 'the deceased woman' had cohabited, he did not know whether they were married. He last saw his brother on 4 August, and was told that he had left the woman and children at Reading according to a prior arrangement – but did not mention the word 'wife' at all. His brother 'and his reputed wife' had visited him at Tunbridge Wells about six weeks earlier, and it was the only time he ever met her. He told John that he was living very unhappily with her, they frequently quarrelled 'on account of her bad temper and ways,' and James was often so upset that he could not concentrate properly on his work. John advised James to separate from her and make her a weekly allowance.

The coroner said that he had no evidence to show that Mrs Legge had been 'a woman of that disposition', and if she was, maybe she had good reason for it 'in the conduct of her husband'. One of the jurors said that according to previous statements, James had got tipsy on their first night away, and could not find his way back to the pub where he had left his family. It was therefore unreasonable 'to cast such a reflection upon the poor woman'. At this John Legge offered to retract his words.

This, the coroner told them, was the end of 'this sad and distressing case'. In summing up, he said the dead woman was 'in the full possession of all her faculties'. There were several extraordinary circumstances, and some of the witnesses' statements had produced contradictory evidence. He personally did not think any crime or murder had been committed, especially as the baby had only been breastfed by his mother a short while before they drowned. Could the jury, he asked, believe that 'at such a moment she would become the destroyer of that child?' There was no evidence of how the deceased came by their deaths, beyond the fact that they had drowned. Was it too far-fetched to assume that it had merely been a tragic accident?

The jury retired for about quarter of an hour, and as there were no marks of violence on any of the bodies, they unanimously returned a verdict of 'found drowned'. Whether they thought it might be uncharitable to accept the view of headline writers who called the case 'murder and suicide' must remain a matter for conjecture.

10

'I WILL DO FOR YOU'

Newbury, 1866

Henry Martin was notorious in Newbury. He had been employed briefly as a butcher's assistant, but was dismissed for cheating a servant girl out of money, and at various times was imprisoned for petty theft. At one stage he moved in with Eliza Shaw, a streetwalker who had a cottage at nearby Woodspeen and had also served several prison sentences for stealing. He managed to live successfully off her ill-gotten gains for some time, until he was sentenced to a month in Reading Gaol for trying to steal a purse from a man at Michaelmas Fair, Newbury.

While in gaol, Martin heard that Shaw had been seen regularly with another man. Her new companion was James Brett, a barman at the Eagle in Bartholomew Street, Newbury. Martin was not a man to take rivals lightly, and moreover, if Eliza had found somebody else, on release he might be faced with the unthinkable – the prospect of having to find a job. Not having to work appealed to him, and he was so infamous in the area that it would be hard to find anyone prepared to consider employing him.

At the beginning of December 1866, Martin was released. After making enquiries, he knew where to find the inconvenient Brett. Eliza had asked her friends to tell Martin that he was not to come near her. If he did, she would sell everything she had, and run away with Brett. However, Martin he would not give her up without a fight. On the evening of 4 December he walked into the Eagle. As expected, he found Brett and Shaw there, both slightly the worse for drink. Martin told Brett in no uncertain terms that he regarded Eliza as his property, and a quarrel broke out. When Martin became verbally abusive, Shaw slapped his face, took hold of his hair, pulled him out of his seat and threw him to the floor. The still-sober Martin knew there were policemen outside, and was careful not to fight back.

Realising the situation could turn even more ugly, the landlady ordered everyone in the pub to leave as quickly as possible. Martin and William Wyatt, whose father was among the policemen outside, were among the last to go. Martin had asked William to fetch him a pickaxe or a hammer, but needless to say William thought better of it and refused. Instead he tried to persuade Martin to come and stay the night under his roof, but Martin declined. He muttered that revenge was sweet, he intended to murder them both, and vowed he would 'not swing for them'.

After shaking William's hand, he wandered off to the cottage at Woodspeen, which he had shared with Eliza before going to gaol. With him he had a butcher's cramp; a steel rod incorporating a hook at one end and a hammer at the other, which had been in his family's possession for nearly a century. As far as he was concerned, prising open the shutters of the cottage was the least of its purposes. Letting himself in, he crept quietly upstairs to the bedroom where Brett and Shaw were sleeping in each other's arms. He seized hold of Brett by the hair, and before the terrified man realised what had hit him, slashed at his throat with a knife. The noise woke Eliza and he hit her several times with the butcher's hook as she screamed, trying in vain to ward off the blows with her hands. Both lay fatally wounded in a pool of blood as Martin made his way out through the window.

Some of the neighbours had heard the noise, but they were so used to Martin and Shaw arguing that the screams seemed nothing to worry about. Meanwhile, Martin had returned to his mother's house at the Rose and Thistle Yard, where he woke her up to say goodbye and tell her that he would never see her again, and then left in pursuit of Messenger, the man whom he had tried to rob but failed. After that, for some unaccountable reason, he returned to the doorstep of Eliza's cottage. She had already died from her wounds, while Brett lingered another few hours. Martin asked some of the neighbours whether they had heard any noise in the night. He then walked into Newbury, while one of Eliza Shaw's neighbours, Elizabeth Goddard, went into the cottage to see for herself. She went upstairs and saw the two naked, blood-soaked bodies; Shaw in bed and Brett lying on the floor still feebly gasping for breath, then went to call the police.

At about 9 a.m. Superintendent Harfield came round to investigate. Shaw had been dead for several hours. She had a wound over her right eyebrow about four inches long, penetrating to the brain, and a fractured skull. Brett was still alive but seriously injured. Dr Silas Palmer was called to see to him, found he had about ten wounds on his face and head, and removed a portion of the bone from the skull, but he died soon after midday.

Meanwhile, Harfield spoke to some of the neighbours, several of whom said they had heard a great deal of noise during the night, though their estimates as to what time varied. Nevertheless, the woman's screams of 'Oh God! Oh God!' followed by male threats of 'I will do for you,' and a thud as someone fell to the floor, were evidence enough. There was no doubt as to the identity of the assailant.

At the coroner's court the jury returned a verdict of wilful murder against Martin, who had gone to the Crown Inn, West Mills, on the south bank of the Kennet and Avon Canal. After a drink he went towards the footbridge at Northcroft, sat down on the bank and took off his hat and boots. He then tied a neck scarf from his pocket around his ankles, and jumped into the freezing water.

Harfield had been told by regulars at the inn where Martin had gone. As he approached the river, a man told him he had seen a body floating downstream. A pair of shoes lay on the towpath. The body was hauled out of the water, and taken to a stable at Enborne to await a coroner's inquest.

In view of what several people in and near Newbury had seen or heard during the previous twenty-four hours, such proceedings were no more than a mere formality. The national and regional newspapers said it all in the heading for their reports, 'DREADFUL MURDER AND SUICIDE NEAR NEWBURY'. They could not resist telling their readers that 'Shaw and Martin were both natives of Newbury, and their characters have been of the worst description.'

At midnight on 6 December, Martin's body was deposited in the churchyard of St Michael's, Enborne, and buried without any Christian rites. The next day the coffins containing the bodies of Shaw and Brett were placed in a cart, covered with a black pall, and drawn from the house to the churchyard at Speen, about a mile away. People had heard in advance of the procession and were standing along the route, largely out of morbid curiosity. The Revd H.W. Magendie addressed the crowd gathered in the churchyard, telling them 'to take warning from the awful events of the past few days.'

11

THE POLICEMEN AND THE POACHERS

Hungerford, 1876

In the nineteenth century, one of the greatest dangers faced by the guardians of law and order was from poachers. On the night of Monday 11 December 1876, Inspector Joseph Drewett and Constable Thomas Shorter were keeping watch at an area north of Hungerford, where poaching was rife. Forty-two-year-old Drewett, who lived at Weston, near Welford, was married with five children, while Shorter, eighteen years younger, was married and lived at Bray, near Maidenhead. They planned to meet at Folly Crossroads.

Constable William Golby, who was on duty at High Street in the town from 10 p.m., was waiting for Inspector Drewett to join him and report on anything he might have noticed while on patrol. He knew Drewett and Shorter usually met at the crossroads, and after waiting a few minutes decided to go and look for them. He was walking up the hill and had reached Denford Bar, when he found a figure lying in the road. At first he assumed it was a drunk who had fallen over, until he went to inspect more closely. To his horror he found it was Shorter, battered to death and lying face downwards in a large pool of blood. He returned to the gatehouse at the entrance to the turnpike to ask the gamekeeper, William Hedges, and his wife to keep an eye out in case anyone should come past, before going back to the police station to report the fate of his colleague. Plans were made for Shorter's body to be removed and a post-mortem examination carried out. The broken lock of a gun was found under Shorter's body.

By now it was shortly after midnight. Constable Charles Brown from Kintbury, who came to help, accompanied Golby on a search for Drewett in the darkness. As they reached Folly Crossroads Golby took the left turning to Chilton Foliat, and

Brown the right turn to Denford. Soon afterwards the latter found the battered body of Inspector Drewett against the bank by the side of Gipsy Lane, about 150 yards away from where Shorter had been found. Striking a match, Brown could just see that Drewett had been shot through the head, probably at point-blank range, and his head badly beaten. He had not drawn his truncheon, and there was nothing to suggest any sign of a struggle with his assailant. His manner of death was presumably similar to that of his colleague. The only sign of any evidence was a mud-stained cap lying nearby.

Meanwhile Superintendent George Bennett was arriving from Newbury with additional police to start a full search of the area. In less than an hour, he learned from Hedges that two men had been through the turnpike gate. They were a labourer, thirty-nine-year-old William Day, thought to be the ringleader of a poaching gang, and his son-in-law, twenty-four-year-old William Tidbury. Both lived in the same row of cottages at Eddington and worked at Cottrell's iron foundry.

Day was eating his breakfast early the next morning when the police came to his cottage to arrest him. Within two hours he had been followed into custody by William Tidbury and his brothers, twenty-six-year-old Henry and seventeen-year-old Francis. In the afternoon all four were brought before Lovelock Cox at the Hungerford police station and formally remanded, and in the evening they were taken to Reading Gaol. A crowd jeered them and for a time there were fears that all four might be lynched.

An inquest on the murdered men was held at the John of Gaunt Inn, Hungerford. The local doctor, Harry Major, established that Drewett had about forty shotgun pellets in a neck wound, but the cause of death was probably severe brain injuries. Shorter had met his death in a similar manner, with every bone in his head broken as a result of the ferocious attack. The two officers had been battered so severely that there was initially doubt as to whether they had been beaten or shot first.

Day and the Tidbury brothers were examined by the local magistrates at several sessions at the Corn Exchange, Hungerford, just before Christmas. Colonel Blandy, the chief constable, led the case for the prosecution, and several witnesses gave evidence against them. Superintendent Bennett described the peculiar nailing of the prisoners' boots, noting that they had corresponded exactly with footprints found on the rain-sodden soil of the fields adjoining Denford Lane and Shefford turnpike road, where the murders were committed. He also pointed out blood marks on the boots and clothes worn by the prisoners when apprehended. On 18 December he was present when Constable Waymen produced a gunstock smeared with blood. He found a broken gunstock among some ivy growing on the ground near the Eddington millstream, within about thirty yards of where the other gunstock was found, and about 100 yards from the prisoners' cottages. The gunstock picked up in the road where Shorter's body was found, and the trigger plate found beneath Drewett's body, both fitted the broken stock, and clearly belonged to the same gun.

Several witnesses remembered seeing the prisoners near the murder scene on the night in question. It was also proved that Day and William Tidbury, talking to different people at different times on the night in question, had each spoken of having another job on hand that night. Sergeant Bull, a superintendent in the Wiltshire Constabulary, spoke of having tracked some footprints across a newly-sown wheatfield from the direction of the scene of the murder, leading towards the prisoners' houses. The footprints were those of somebody who had been running, and corresponded with the boots of Francis George Tidbury, the youngest of the prisoners. In the prisoner's house he later found a bloodstained axe handle. At this point Day's wife, standing in the crowd, shouted out, 'That stick was used to kill a rabbit with.'

Frederick Hughes, a moulder employed at the Eddington ironworks, testified to the correctness of the wax castings of the footprints, produced by Superintendent Bennett.

Thomas Briant, who lived in one of the cottages at Picket Lot, near where the murders took place, said he fetched his daughter Elizabeth from Hungerford on Monday night, and arrived at his home in Denford Lane at 10.25 p.m. She had to go out to the back of the cottage for something, and when she came back she told him she had heard some men pass by, saying she thought they were some of the Tidbury family, whom she knew to be poachers. Next morning he found a policeman's helmet about ten yards from Shorter's body.

Hungerford High Street.

Inspector Joseph Drewett.

William Hedges, keeper of the turnpike gate at Eddington Hill, said that he and his wife were called up on the night of 11 December by Constable Golby, who told them what had happened, and asked them to notice who was down the road. As they kept watch they saw the prisoners, William Day and William Tidbury, coming towards the gate. When he spoke to them, he noticed they were both shivering. They told him they had been standing about a long time, then they wished him goodnight, and continued down the lane towards their homes. His wife corroborated her husband's evidence, and said Day told her they had been up to see Mr Piggott at Hidden Farm, to put a plug in an engine. He also asked her if she was staying up to let Mr Piggott through the gate. Afterwards she went to call on a neighbour, and as she made a noise at the door she saw Day and William Tidbury quicken their pace in the direction of their cottages.

Constable Brown mentioned being told of Shorter's murder by Constable Golby, and their going together in search of Drewett's body, which they found in Denford Lane. After they had put the body in a cart, a cloth cap was found at the site where the body had been lying. At about 10.30, three hours before meeting Golby, he had heard a gun being fired while on duty near Eleat Lodge. The cap picked up in Denford Lane was shown to Amos Batt, who said he had just seen a man wearing one like it as he went through the turnpike gate on the Monday night.

John Hancocke, foreman at the Eddington Ironworks Foundry, confirmed that the three Tidburys were employed there. He spoke to a pale and agitated Henry Tidbury about the murder next morning, and Henry asked to be allowed to visit the place, but Hancocke would not let him leave his work. He knew that the cap produced by police belonged to Henry Tidbury, as he recognised it from the grease on it, by its general appearance, and by a particular button. Henry had been wearing it until Monday evening, but on Tuesday he came to work in a billycock, or felt hat, a detail confirmed by Thomas Redgate, another foreman at the foundry.

Sergeant Wiltshire stated that when the blood marks on the prisoners' clothes were shown to them at the station, Day said he had been rabbiting, and the marks on his gaiters were through catching rabbits.

Constable Thomas Shorter.

BRUTAL MURDER!!
In Berkshire.

On Monday, December 11th, Inspector Drewitt, and P. C. Shorter were found murdered on the high road, one mile from Hungerford. Four desperate Poachers are in custody for the crime.

Tune—Driven from Home.

A barbarous murder on the country road side,
All throughout Berkshire is spread far and wide ;
An Inspector of police, and a private as well,
Both have been murdered, we're sorry to tell.
Upon Monday night their bodies were found
By another Policeman on his lonely round ;
When near Dewford toll-bar a sight met his gaze,
He'll never forget to the end of his days.

CHORUS.

Near Hungerford, in Berkshire, on a lonely road
    side,
Two Policemen by a murder so cruel they died ;
Quite dead and cold they were both of them found,
Their brains beaten out as they lay on the ground.

A more unmanly crime has seldom been known,
I am sure you will say if your hearts are not stone,
To take poor men's lives in cold blood we must say,
Is not like an Englishman's love of fair play ;
They must have been beaten to death on the ground,
Till the blood of the victims in pools lay around !
They gave them no chance their lives to defend,
The unequall struggle soon came to an end.

The eleventh of December, a dark gloomy night;
The two men were found, what a sad ghastly sight !
By the police of the district the alarm was soon
    spread,
Much sympathy was shown for the poor murdered
    dead.

Four men were taken with blood on their clothes,
Whether they are guilty God only knows !
We will not condemn, tho' they bear a bad name,
f they are the murderers so much to their shame.

Two of the men who are taken, they say,
Must have passed down the road where the two
    bodies lay ;
The man at the toll gate saw them go through.
He watch'd for their coming as he'd been told to do ;
They seem'd agitated and hurried along,
Suspicion against them has been very strong ;
Let us take care that none but the guilty shall fall,
Tho' this world's full of trouble, life's dear to us all.

Four men are charged with this cruel crime,
The charge they must answer at the proper time ;
Two men have been killed, and justice will say,
The murderers we know cannot be far away.
Blood for blood has long been the law of the land,
And in crimes that are done with a cowardly hand,
It is nothing but right such men should be taught
The revenge of a murderer is too dearly bought.

These Policemen, no doubt, have left children and
    wives,
Who are plunged in a sorrow that will last them
    their lives ;
They will never forget where'er they may roam,
The night when they brought these poor murdered
    men home.
Their prospects in future are blighted and gone,
We hope they're not friendless altho' they're alone,
As they stand by the grave of those they love best,
May their prayers be heard for the dear ones at rest.

London :—H. P. SUCH, Machine Printer and Publisher, 177, Union-street, Borough.

A ballad lamenting the murder of both men.

Samuel Hawkes, a barber in Hungerford, said that Henry Tidbury was in his shop on Friday 1 December when they were talking about poaching and about a recent murder at Yeovil. He told the witness he had killed nine pheasants in one night, and that there was no fear of keepers coming when a gun was fired, as he could not tell how many poachers there were. During the conversation Henry said that if a keeper came up to him he would 'shoot him or rip him up, rather than be took', a statement which not surprisingly produced some surprise in court. He also said he would not kill a policeman or anyone else he knew, but that he 'would punish them' before they could arrest him. Arthur Cork, a freelance printer, was in Mr Hawkes' shop at the same time and corroborated evidence on the conversation. Tidbury spoke about the number of pheasants he had poached one night in the neighbourhood. Hawkes, who was cutting Tidbury's hair at the time, asked him if he was not afraid, to which the reply was, 'No, I am not afraid of meeting a keeper in a copse at night.' When Hawkes caught hold of Tidbury by the back of the head, and asked him what he would do if any one attempted to take him like that, Tidbury said that if he was a stranger he would shoot the man rather than be caught, but if it was a policeman or a keeper whom he knew, he would punch him.

Henry Tidbury admitted to talking about the pheasants, but insisted he never said a word about killing anybody. Such testimony 'seemed got up to make it worse for him'; the witnesses responsible would only make it worse for their own souls, and he was prepared to take an oath before God and man that he never said such a thing. Hawkes said he was sure Henry used the language repeated. William Winkworth, of Hungerford, said that early in December he heard Day say he would smash anybody who tried to take him into custody. He also spoke of two gamekeepers, employed respectively on the Denford and Chorlton Lodge estates, said their time was short, and told Winkworth that he would shortly hear something.

Mrs Gibbs of Denford said she had heard gunshots in one of the nearby woods between 9 and 10 p.m. on the night of the murders. Day and two of the Tidburys said they were at work at that time, and Francis Tidbury did not comment on the evidence. Ralph Waller, landlord of the Oxford Arms, Hungerford, said that at just after 10 p.m. he heard a shot fired that seemed to come from the woods just over half a mile from his house.

About a week after Christmas, Colonel Blandy reported to Berkshire Quarter Sessions that Drewett had been seventeen years in the force. The Police Committee recommended that a gratuity of one year's pay, £91 5s, should be paid to his widow. Shorter had served two years, and had only subscribed for that period to the superannuation fund, so his widow was not eligible for any grant.

When the case before the magistrates resumed on 5 January, further witnesses were called. The prisoners' bloodstained clothes had been sent to London on 23 December to an analytical chemist for examination. Dr Harry Major, the Hungerford surgeon, said that on the Thursday after the murder he examined their clothes and boots, and found them stained with blood. On some of them marks of red lead were visible, and also some whiting or white powder, and there was evidence of an attempt having been made to scrape the blood marks off the clothes.

Superintendent Bennett proved that Day had red lead on his hands when apprehended, and there were marks of red lead on his clothes, but no such marks on the bed where he was said to have slept. Day's clothes, particularly his breeches, were heavily marked with red lead, and appeared to have been scraped to erase the marks. Bloodstains were discernible under the red lead marks when placed under a magnifying glass. He traced fresh footprints on the ground between the prisoners' cottages and the stream at Eddington on the day after the murder, past the spot where the two gunstocks were discovered, and said he was sure they were William Day's footsteps. There was blood on the briers of the hedge, where a tobacco box thought to be Day's was found.

Sergeant Bull of the Wiltshire Police corroborated Bennett's evidence as to Day's footprints between the house of the prisoners and the millstream near where the gunstocks were discovered, and also as to the blood and brains being on the briers near the Inspector's body where the tobacco box was discovered.

William Bailey, an engine driver from Ogborne St George, confirmed that the gunstocks found near the prisoners' cottages both belonged to Henry Tidbury. One was from a gun he had sold Henry at Michaelmas. He also identified the lock and trigger-plate produced as belonging to the same gun. Bailey also identified the second gunstock found by the police as part of a weapon which a Mr William Talbot had sold Henry Tidbury for 5s five years earlier, when he (Bailey) lived near Henry Tidbury. Having seen the gun so many times, he 'could swear to it among a thousand'. The complete gun produced belonged to William Day. Bailey found the gun in Mr Piggott's hedge at the Hidden Farm on one occasion, and took it to Piggott, for whom he was then working, and Day abused him fiercely for having taken the gun to Piggott.

Several other witnesses were called at this hearing, which proved to be the final examination on 12 January. One, Professor Charles Tidy, of the London Hospital, stated that on 23 December he had received from Superintendent Bennett a sealed box containing four bundles of clothes labelled with the names of William, Francis and Henry Tidbury, and William Day. Bennett pointed out the suspicious stains, which he removed for examination. He had inspected the clothes and found bloodstains on some of the clothes of William and Francis Tidbury, though not on their boots, and none on the clothes of Henry Tidbury. There was blood on the leggings and coat of William Day, but none on his other garments.

Tidy could not confirm how old the bloodstains were, but thought they were very recent, and he could not say whether the blood was human or otherwise. Apart from two spots on William Tidbury's left legging the stains were small smears, and not of any definite shape. There were scratches on the clothes as if water had been used to eradicate the blood spots, and that would have given them the appearance of smears.

Sergeant Robert Butcher of the Berkshire Police had been in charge of the prisoners at the remand hearings. While in the train with them between Hungerford and Newbury after the examination on 15 December, he reported, Day told the others that he would speak up for himself:

> I'm innocent; you know you three done it. What did you leave me on this farm for? When we came down the road, why did you say it was a drunken man lying in the road, and we had better not take notice of him, when you knowed who it was all the while, and that you done it. Didn't you come in the morning and say if any one asked me about the man we saw in the road last night I was to know nothing about it. You know you did, if you speaks the truth. You can't deny it. If I am hung, it will be through you three, and you know it.

He did not hear any reply from the Tidbury brothers to these remarks. Day and Henry Tidbury left the train at Newbury in charge of the police, while William and Francis Tidbury were taken on to Reading. After the train had left Newbury, Butcher remarked to the Tidburys, 'Bill Day is making it rather warm for you, if that's true.' William answered, 'You don't know so much about Day as I do.' Nothing more was said by the prisoners.

Constable Brown said that while in charge of Henry Tidbury on 5 January, after he had been in court, Henry said to him, 'Brown, I have never blamed you for anything.' He then said that the cap Brown had was his, 'I was there, and I am a guilty man.' Brown said, 'All you have to do is prepare to meet your maker,' to which Henry answered, 'I am trying to do so.'

Day denied any part in the murder, stating that he and William Tidbury went to Mr Crook's, at Hidden Farm, to repair an engine, and after that William went to take some things to the farmhouse he had had while at work. He said he heard guns fired, and on his way home he caught up with William Tidbury in the road. As they went towards Hungerford, he saw something lying in the road, and asked what it was, William urged him to carry on, saying it was only a drunken man. He wanted to go back and check, but William urged him to go home. Until then he had not seen Henry or Francis, and nothing was said about what had happened. In the morning Henry Tidbury came into his house and said to his wife, 'You tell Bill that if anyone asks him if he saw any one as he was coming home last night he must say no.'

William Tidbury's statement corroborated everything Day had said. He added that while Day had gone to take the things back to the farm he heard two guns fired, and ran across the park and heard someone call, 'Oh dear, what shall I do?' He cried out, 'Who's there?' and his brother Harry called out, 'Is that you, Bill?' He said it was. His brother then put his hand on his arm, and said, 'Bill, I've killed two policemen,' then added that he had lost his hat. William told him it was too dark to find it, and he ought to go home. It was hard, William added, to tell on his own brother, but he was so frightened that he did not know what to do with himself. Henry and Francis went on to Hungerford, and then William Day arrived. As the brothers saw the man lying in the road, William thought it was one of the policemen, and told Day to come on. When Superintendent Bennett apprehended him the next morning he told a lie to protect his brother, but he was certainly not present when the murder was committed.

The other two prisoners, Henry and Francis Tidbury, declined to make any statement, and all four were committed for trial at the Spring Assizes at Reading. Later that day it was later reported that during an interview with his relations, Henry confessed to his mother that he and Francis had been involved in the murder. Henry himself shot Drewett, and Francis assisted in beating him.

The trial opened at Berkshire Assizes before Mr Justice Lindley on 19 February 1877. Such large crowds gathered outside the court before proceedings opened that the officials had to make it admission by ticket only, and police had to be called to control them. The prisoners pleaded not guilty to both charges of murder. Mr Griffiths, Recorder of Reading, was counsel for the prosecution, while Montagu Williams defended Day and William Tidbury, and Baker Smith undertook the defence of Henry and Francis Tidbury.

The murder of Shorter was dealt with first. Over forty witnesses were called, the majority of whom had already given evidence at the earlier hearings. On the second day of proceedings, Griffiths submitted that the amount of force used against the police officers was such that it could not have been exercised by two persons, and therefore all four prisoners had probably been involved in the murders. Was not the great body of evidence given against the prisoners enough, he asked, to convince them of the prisoners' guilt?

Baker Smith argued on behalf of Henry and Francis Tidbury that the police officers themselves could have been the assailants, and if so the prisoners were only acting in self-defense. Montagu Williams then submitted on behalf of Day and William Tidbury that had they taken part in the murder they would surely have made off for their homes across the fields, and not been so rash as to go past the tollkeeper and his wife, who would undoubtedly have recognised them. As for the blood on Day's clothes, he suggested that this was rabbit and not human blood.

Henry Tidbury confessed that he and Francis were responsible for the killings, and that when the shooting took place the other two were out of the woods. While returning home with two pheasants, they were stopped by Drewett who had recognised them, and Henry shot him to avoid being arrested. Shorter then arrived, Francis shot at him but Shorter dodged the bullet, ran back down the lane and along the road in the direction of Hungerford. They overtook him, shot him again and battered him to death, then walked over to the still-conscious Drewett. He begged them to spare him, but they battered him where he lay until they were satisfied he was dead.

The Inspector Drewett memorial cross, near Folly Cross. (© Simon Dell)

The Constable Shorter memorial cross, near Folly Cross. (© Simon Dell)

Left and below: *The grave of Inspector Drewett and Constable Shorter, Hungerford cemetery (© Simon Dell)*

At the end of the day the jury retired at 7.15 p.m. and returned at 9.30. They found William Day not guilty of murdering Shorter. William Tidbury, they said, was not guilty of the murder either, but he was an accessory after the murder was committed, but recommended him to mercy on the grounds that he was shielding his guilty brothers. Francis and Henry Tilbury they found guilty, but recommended mercy in Francis's case as the killing was unpremeditated, and on account of his youth. Nevertheless, the judge sentenced Francis and Henry to hang.

On 21 February a fresh jury was sworn in, and William Day and William Tidbury were charged with the murder of Drewett. Griffiths said that he and his colleague Mr Greene proposed to offer no evidence on the charge, and were prepared to allow a verdict of acquittal. Both prisoners were discharged, to the sounds of applause from their friends in court, which was immediately suppressed. A public petition requesting the reduction of Francis Tidbury's sentence to one of life imprisonment received 1,400 signatures in one day on the grounds that he had been acting under the influence of Henry, but it was rejected. The brothers were executed at Reading Gaol by William Marwood on the morning of 12 March, Francis's eighteenth birthday. After the executions, copies of confessions they had made were passed to the press.

William Marwood, executioner between 1872 and 1883.

The policemen had been popular in the area, and there was much anger and sadness at their violent deaths. A public subscription raised a generous sum for their widows and families. They were buried in Eddington churchyard, close to where they had been killed, and memorial crosses were erected beside the road where the bodies were found. In 1996 one of the crosses was stolen and replaced, but the replacement itself was damaged in 2003. A representative of Thames Valley Police had two crosses cast from the remaining original, and they were unveiled at a special dedication ceremony on 9 January 2004. It was decided that the surviving original would be mounted at Hungerford police station.

12

THE BUTCHER'S APPRENTICE

Slough, 1881

At the beginning of 1881, one of the most respected and well-established businesses in Windsor Road, Slough, was the butcher's shop run by Hezekiah and Ann Reville. Husband and wife ran the business with the aid of two apprentices, fourteen-year-old Philip Glass and sixteen-year-old Alfred Payne, both of whom had been working for them for a couple of years.

The only major problem they had was pilfering. For some months meat had been vanishing from the shop, and the Revilles were fairly certain they knew where it was going. It was said that meat was being sold off at bargain prices outside the Royal Oak, Slough, an inn run by Payne's father. Cautious by nature, Hezekiah wanted to be sure of his facts before dismissing Payne for theft, especially as Mr Payne was a well-respected local businessman, and he had no desire to fall out with him if it could be avoided. Ann thought they would save themselves a good deal of difficulties if they just asked the troublesome youth to leave. With some reluctance Hezekiah asked Mrs Glass, Philip's mother, if she could possibly use her discretion to ask her son how Payne was managing to remove the joints from the shop. Ill-feeling was increasing between the surly Payne and Mrs Reville, and it would be as well for them all if they could resolve the issue as soon and as satisfactorily as possible.

It was soon to be resolved – but in the worst possible way. After close of business on 11 April 1881 Hezekiah left Ann in the shop, working on the books, while he went to have a quiet drink with friends down the road. Payne and Glass were also still in the shop, washing down counters for the next day's work, though Payne did so with the reluctant air of one who had been spoken to by his employer, or employer's wife, in a way which he resented.

Chalvey High Street. (Land Collection)

Glass left for his home at about 6.30 p.m., leaving Payne to continue on his own. About two hours later George Roll, a bricklayer walking home, passed Payne outside the shop. He thought that the youth seemed in a hurry, and this was confirmed by another person, Kate Timms, who passed him in the High Street a few minutes later. At about 8.45 p.m. one of Ann Reville's friends, their next-door neighbour Eliza Beasley, came to the shop to visit her. As she looked in through the window she saw Ann sitting in a chair facing the window, a book open on the desk. At first she thought she had fainted, but after seeing the injuries on her neck, and rightly fearing the worst she immediately summoned the police and a doctor. Surgeon Mr Dodd was the first to arrive.

Soon afterwards the stunned Hezekiah Reville, having been sent a message at the inn, came back accompanied by Sergeant Hobbs from the Slough Police. At about 9 o'clock Superintendent Dunham arrived to take charge of what had just become a murder enquiry. Suspicion fell at first on the widower, but it was soon evident that husband and wife had been on the best of terms, and it was beyond doubt that he had been absent from the shop at the time of her death.

Nothing, it appeared, had been stolen, which ruled out robbery as the motive. A meat cleaver was found lying beside the body, under which Mr Dodd found a piece of paper on which was scrawled:

Mrs Reville, – You will never sell me no more bad meat like you did on Saturday. I told Mrs Austin, at Chalvey, that I would do for her. I done it for the bad meat she sold me on Saturday last. H. Collins, Colnbrook.

Dunham asked Reville if he had a customer of that name at Colnbrook. He admitted that he had, though he was sure the man had never been sold bad meat, would have never written a note in that style, and in any case the handwriting was nothing like his. Then the problems with Payne were mentioned, and Dunham decided he probably needed to look no further for the culprit. After a thorough search of the house he went to the Royal Oak to see Payne's father, who called his son out and asked him what time he had left the Revilles' premises. The boy answered that it was a few minutes after 8 o'clock, and that he had left Mrs Reville there.

'Do you know she is murdered?' asked Dunham. 'No,' was the reply. 'Do you know where the chopper was?' asked Dunham. Payne said he saw the chopper on the block, and a knife near the weights and scale.

Dunham apprehended Payne and took him to the police station for questioning. The boy was also asked to write his name and various other things so that the police had an example of his handwriting. When asked, he repeatedly insisted that he had left the shop at 8.30 the previous evening, and that Mrs Reville was alive and well at the time.

The inquest opened that same day at the Crown Inn, High Street, under Frederick Charsley, coroner for South Buckinghamshire. Evidence on the pilfering from the shop, and on the difficult atmosphere between the murdered woman and Payne, was given by Mrs Glass and her son as well as by Hezekiah Reville. Philip Glass said Mr Reville had left the premises at 8.10 p.m., and he himself had been there until 8.25 p.m. He said he was unaware of any disagreements, but had heard Mrs Reville speak to Payne on occasions, yet he had never heard Payne utter any threats. About a month earlier he understood Payne was going to give notice to leave, but Mr Reville asked him to stay.

In his evidence, Mr Reville said that he had had occasion to complain of Payne's attitude and work. He spent more time in the public house than attending to his business, leaving most of the work to Glass. Though Payne improved after being spoken to, he still tended to neglect his duties and arrive late, and he had heard his wife complain about Payne on Saturday night, two days before the murder. He had found a piece of steak concealed under a blade-bone, and although he must have known who was responsible, he remarked that he would like to find out who the thief was.

'Ah, you'll never do that,' his wife remarked. 'You have not seen half that I have.'

As Mr Reville left the shop, he noticed Payne writing on a piece of paper. He told Mrs Glass that he was going to dismiss Payne, as his wife had told him that if he did not, then she would. One of the customers had warned her she ought to keep an eye on Payne, and after that she made a point of putting any loose money in her pocket instead of leaving it lying around. Payne had noticed, realised he was under suspicion, and thereon there had been a change in his attitude towards his employers for the worse.

After Eliza Beasley described how she found Mrs Reville, Payne was brought into court. On being duly cautioned by the coroner that anything he might say would be taken down and used against him if necessary, he said:

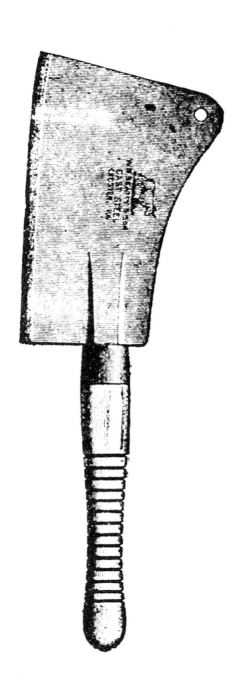
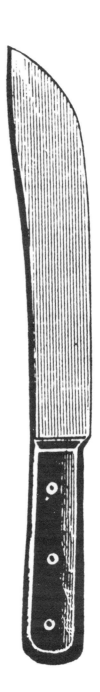

I've only got to say that Mrs Reville was sitting at the books when I came out of the door. She said 'Good night' to me, and asked me to shut the door. I asked her if I should shut the door. She said, 'No, turn the gas down and leave the door open.' The tools were all laid together on the block when I came out except the knife, and that laid against the weights and scale. It was 8.32 when I came out of the door, and I made straight home. I looked at the clock. That's all I've got to say. I don't want to say any more.

Sergeant Hobbs said he was coming up the High Street at about 8.45 p.m., and after being told what had happened he went straight to see Mr Reville. The deceased had been sitting in a chair, facing the window, with a ledger in front of her open at entries for 19 March. He noticed a large wound on the right side of the neck, and two others on the head. There was much blood around, most of it still wet. On the ground he found a pen, and behind Mrs Reville a table, on which was a chopper with blood and hair and some papers resting on top, while on the table was the note near the chopper, and there were splashes of blood on the cloth and on the floor. Robert Collins of Chalvey was there to deny ever having received bad meat, and also confirmed that he did not write the note (which had been signed 'H. Collins', not 'R. Collins'). Mr Payne, Alfred's father, was putting no obstacles in the way of the enquiry, and when questioned by the coroner, said he was not at home when his son returned.

There was not enough evidence to justify holding Payne, and he was released. His conduct at the shop had been a cause of regular complaint by his employers, and the ill will he bore towards them as a result placed him under suspicion, but this was insufficient to charge him with any offence.

Payne never denied leaving the shop at 8.30, and additional evidence of the fact was provided by Kate Timms and George Roll. Mrs Beasley described the discovery of her friend's body, and Mr Dodd gave a full account of her injuries, confirmed by the police surgeon, Mr Bute. Dunham told the court that the note found under Mrs Reville was 'ridiculous', but just to cover all available ground, he had interviewed Collins and found there was no possibility of it being written by him. He also said that the 'confession' had been written on a notebook belonging to Payne, and the half-sheet of paper on which it was written corresponded to a half-sheet still in the book. Charles Chabot, a handwriting expert called to examine the writing, said that he had been given examples of Payne's writing but needed time to study them, a request Mr Charsley readily granted.

After a two-hour adjournment, Chabot returned to tell them that he had found at least fifteen different similarities between the handwriting of Payne and Collins's alleged confession. He admitted that it was not an exact science, but he was as certain as he could be that Payne was the writer of the note.

Payne took the stand briefly, and repeated that he and the Revilles had been on the best of terms. If they were looking for a murderer, he said, maybe they should ask some of the tramps in the area. However, it was pointed out that any tramp would almost certainly have stolen something whilst in the shop. The jury were out for two hours and, with one dissenter out of fourteen, returned a verdict of wilful murder against Payne, who was taken to Aylesbury to await trial at the assizes.

Ann Reville's funeral was held at St Mary's Church on the afternoon of 14 April, the service being taken by the Revd P.W. Phipps, vicar of Slough. Much sympathy was expressed for the widower of the twenty-five-year-old woman, and their two children, aged five and three respectively.

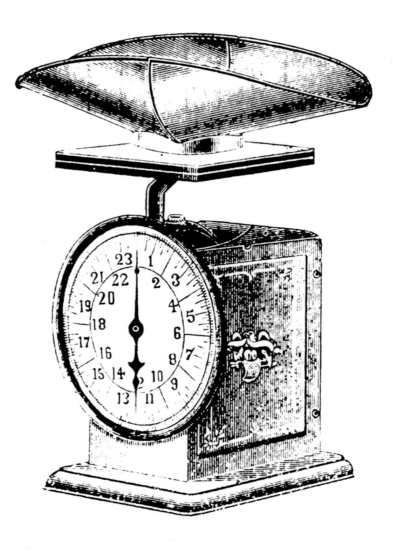

The trial opened on 28 April 1881 at Aylesbury, under Mr Justice Lopes, with John Compton Lawrance, QC (and Conservative MP for South Lincolnshire) and Mr Bullock, counsel for the prosecution, and Walter Attenborough for the defence. Dunham said that Payne's motives were plainly theft and fear of dismissal, and he had been alone with Mrs Reville for nearly two hours after close of business. There was strong circumstantial evidence of the page from the notebook, and Chabot's testimony regarding the handwriting.

On the second day of the trial, in a persuasive summing up, Attenborough contended that according to the evidence, eight minutes had elapsed between Payne leaving the shop and the discovery of Mrs Reville's body, thus leaving ample time for a stranger to enter the premises and commit the murder. As for the letter, it was not shown that Payne had any knowledge of the name of Mr Collins by whom it purported to be signed, and the handwriting analysis was purely speculative, showing as it did similarities with Mr Reville's own writing. It was also pointed out that the dead woman's pocket had been rifled of a few shillings. When Payne was arrested, no money was found on him, although if he had taken anything from her he would have had ample time to put it somewhere else, and no trace of blood was found on his clothes.

Largely on these two factors, and perhaps also in view of his tender years, Payne walked free. The jury retired to deliberate for half an hour, and returned a verdict of not guilty. The police and public, who had been firmly convinced of his guilt, were astounded. Nobody else was questioned, let alone arrested, in connection with the murder. Officially the case remains unsolved, but the general opinion was that young Payne had been extremely lucky in having Mr Attenborough to conduct his defence.

13

THE COAL DEALER AND THE POACHER

Chalvey, 1888

Seven years after the murder of Ann Reville, the community of Slough was horrified by another murder. Several people who had been involved in the investigation and trial of Alfred Payne in 1881 played similar roles again, and by coincidence the outcome proved to be remarkably similar.

Fifty-seven-year-old Charles Dance, a coal dealer from Chalvey, near Slough, and his wife Harriet lived next door to the Foresters Arms, a property he rented from Mr Hines, and he employed a full-time worker, Mr Higgins, as well as seasonal part-time help. Dance tended to carry large sums of money around with him in a small black saddlebag, as he visited local hostelries where he did much of his business. Although he had often been warned by family and friends that this was risky, he assured them that he would come to no harm.

On 21 December he was going to the Garibaldi Inn to collect some club money. Higgins had planned to join him, and came to call for him at about 8 p.m. When he knocked at the front door, Mrs Dance told him that her husband was still out on business. A few minutes later Mrs Dance was interrupted again, this time by William James. He had worked for them in the past, but they suspected he was stealing ducks and other edible fowl from the smallholding which they ran behind their coal business. At one stage they told Constable Horne, who had found James sleeping in Charles's tool shed, and also discovered feathers in a box at the quarry where James had found another job, in November. They decided not to press charges and the theft of chickens stopped for a while, but recently it had started again. Dance had taken to the occasional all-night vigil, sleeping in the shed as a deterrent to the light-fingered party responsible. Now, James came to the house to tell 'Uncle Charles' that a man was looking for him. Resenting the familiarity as this slippery youth was certainly not their nephew, she opened the window and told him coldly that Mr Dance was not there. James asked her to tell him when he returned that the man would see him at the Foresters Arms. 'Try the Garibaldi,' she shouted as he walked off.

Later he said he had left his lodgings at Mrs Moody's at about 8 p.m., gone to the laundry where his mother worked and talked to her for a few minutes, then went outside and met a man who was asking for Charles Dance. The man, he said, aged about forty, was wearing an overcoat and soft felt hat, and had a dog with him. He had seen the man around before in Eton and Slough, had taken him to Dance's premises and made enquiries as to the latter's whereabouts, but with no result. The man was never traced.

Mrs Sarah Moody was James's landlady, and he owed her arrears of 8s for four weeks' rent. On 19 December she had asked him rather testily to pay up, and he had promised her he would do so by the Friday, three days later. The day had now come, and as he was about to go out she felt justified in reminding him yet again. He told her that he was about to draw his Christmas money from the White Hart that evening, and he would then be in a position to pay her in full.

Having left the house at 6.15, he returned at 7.30, appearing not quite his usual self, went into the dining room and took off his jacket. Next he took off his boots and put them on the open fire, then turned to Mrs Moody and asked her that, if anybody asked where he had been, she must tell them that he did not go out until after 8 p.m. He then washed, took an old coat from his room and walked out of the house again, returning a couple of hours later to find Mr and Mrs Moody waiting for him. They were expecting further excuses for non-payment of rent, but James handed them 1s 6d, saying the White Hart had paid him 30s. He had spent some of it drinking with a local prostitute, who was known as 'Whoops my darlin'', and had a 10s note which he hoped to break the next day, and would then discharge his debts.

The Garibaldi
Inn, Chalvey.

Meanwhile, Mrs Dance was becoming increasingly concerned at her husband's failure to return home, as he was rarely late. Mr Higgins agreed to go and check the local public houses, returning just before midnight to say that they had all been closed for a while and there was no sign of her husband. By about 5 a.m. she could bear it no more and went to see Higgins again. He had retired for the night, but agreed to continue looking, and concentrate his search elsewhere. First he went to Dance's tool shed, and on shining his torch inside he saw a dark liquid on the door handle, which on closer inspection turned out to be blood. Moving his torch further over the smallholding, he saw the beaten and battered body of Charles Dance, lying dead across an upturned wheelbarrow.

Higgins at once sent for the police, and informed Mrs Dance of the terrible news. An inquest was opened that morning under Mr Charsley at the Cape of Good Hope Inn with Higgins, Mrs Dance, and the police surgeon William Buee all giving evidence. The latter spoke of the dead man's injuries: a wound on the mouth, a broken jaw, and a cheek torn open, exposing a small gap of flesh. Mr Dance also had a cut hand and a broken finger where he had tried to ward off the attacker's blows, which were thought to have been from a sledgehammer. His skull was fractured and there was a loss of blood from the blow to his face. The surgeon thought he had choked to death on his own blood after being beaten.

The next day, Christmas Eve, Superintendent Dunham arrested William James, who was brought up at Slough Petty Sessions Court before the chairman Springall Thompson. At the proceedings, Mrs Sarah Moody told the Court of the prisoner's suspicious behaviour on the night of 22 December, of his going out at 6.15 and returning at 7.50, the fact that he had put his boots to burn on the fire and changed his jacket, later found to be bloodstained, his warning her to say that he had not gone out before 8 p.m., his washing, and the money he had obtained. When he handed over the 1s 6d, she noticed that he had several notes on him. She mentioned that there had been blood in the sink where he was washing, and also in the drains outside that she and a neighbour had had to wash away with several bucketfuls of water. Next she told the court that he had gone out early on Saturday morning, and returned about 10 a.m. to find the drains being washed down. He asked them lightheartedly what they were doing, then told them that Mr Dance was dead, and that the police had picked up his jacket. Then he turned to Mrs Moody, pointed at her and reminded her to remember that he did not go out until after 8 o'clock the previous evening. After this evidence the enquiry was adjourned.

On 28 December Mr Dance's funeral took place at St Peter's Church, his coffin being followed by a large number of mourners. That same day the hearing resumed at the Cape of Good Hope Inn. The coroner, Mr Charsley, said that since they had last met he thought it his duty to have the prisoner arrested upon his warrant. For the prosecution Mr Brummell-Smith recalled Mrs Moody, who repeated much of her

St Peter's Church, Chalvey.
(© Nigel Cox)

evidence, notably about the bloodstains seen on James's coat and trousers, as well as on the sink and the towel he had used.

Proceedings had to be adjourned a second time, as the prosecution needed to wait for the results of forensic tests on the clothing and other articles. These arrived on 9 January 1889 but proved inconclusive. Mr W.W. Fisher, the public analyst for Berkshire, Buckinghamshire and Oxfordshire, said he had taken samples from a hat, coat, trousers, towel and moneybag provided by Superintendent Dunham. There were bloodstains on the coat and trousers, but the clothes had been washed, and he could not say for certain whether the stains were from human or animal blood.

This counted in James's favour, as did the testimony of Mr Bull, a Chalvey surgeon, who had treated James for an injury to his right wrist a few days earlier. The sledgehammer blows to Mr Dance's face had probably been inflicted with the right hand and with great force, and he said he did not think James would have been strong enough to inflict them until his wrist had healed completely.

Next in the witness box was Superintendent Dunham. He described the discovery of Dance's body, saying he was sure the murder had taken place in the shed, and that the body had been dragged outside. It was the same shed in which James had often slept, and on the smallholding where he had been suspected of stealing fowl. He also recounted in detail an interview he had had with James on the afternoon of 23 December. James had told him he did not go out until 8 p.m. on 22 December, but Mrs Moody had refuted this.

The next three witnesses did little to help James's case. Thomas Austin, a gardener, said he had met James at 7.20 on the evening of 22 December and James borrowed 2*d* from him, claiming he did not have the price of a pint. Now James asked Austin if he was sure it had been 7.20 and not 8.20 when they met. Austin was positive, as he had been home by 7.45.

Next came James Catherwood, landlord of the White Hart. He said James had not withdrawn any money from his slate club on 22 December. James had been a member but defaulted in April, eight months earlier, drawing out the small amount already accumulated, and had not even been in the inn on Friday night. He was followed by James Henry Swain of Rose Cottage, High Street, Chalvey, who said he had been out walking his dog near the Foresters Arms on 22 December between 7.20 and 7.30 p.m., when he saw a tall man climbing the fence at the coal yard, and the description he gave fitted that of James. When asked why he had not reported it to the police at once, he said he thought it was just some poor man getting himself a chicken for Christmas. On being shown James's coat, Swain said he was sure it was the same one worn by the man climbing the fence, as he noticed the colour and cut clearly by the lamplight near the Foresters Arms.

Alfred Glass, landlord of the Flags, said that James had arrived shortly after 8 p.m., and asked for a pint of beer, which he paid for with two penny coins. Twenty minutes later he was joined by 'Whoops my darlin''. When Mr Tompson asked the lady's correct name, Mr Glass said he did not know, as she had been known by her nickname for some years. He then went on to describe how James had bought her several Irish whiskies and glasses of ale, and must have spent between 6s and 7s altogether than evening. It struck Glass as unusual for James to be so free and easy with his cash, when in the past he had known others obtain her favours by spending far less. This provoked such laughter in the court that Tompson found it necessary to call everyone to order. He reminded Glass that he was there merely to give firm evidence and not indulge in speculation. As there were no more questions, he could now stand down.

The jury returned a verdict of wilful murder against William James, who was remanded in custody and went on trial on 2 February 1889 at Aylesbury. Judge Sir James Fitzjames-Stephens presided, with Mr Bonsley and Mr Percival-Keep for the prosecution, Walter Attenborough and Mr Lindell for the defence. James seemed to be quite unconcerned throughout.

Attenborough had conducted a skilful defence of Alfred Payne during the Reville murder trial in 1881, and he was to do the same again for his client almost eight years later. He produced as witnesses Ann and James Stanley. Ann testified under oath that James had brought her two fowl at 7.30 p.m. on 22 December, and she paid him for them and two other birds he had previously given her. He had obviously been poaching, she said, as there was blood on his hands and jacket. James Stanley said he had returned home at 8 p.m. and seen the same fowl on his draining board in the kitchen. This statement was extremely helpful for James, as was evidence from surgeon Mr Bull, who proved that Dance's body must have been dragged about six yards, probably with the aid of a rope or harness, as James had lost his belt. It would have been impossible, said Bull, for a man with an injured wrist – as James had – to drag a heavy body that distance.

Attenborough based his defence on the Stanleys' testimony. He could find a plausible answer, he said, for every suspicious action of the prisoner. It all became clear if one bore in mind that he had been poaching. He pointed out that on the night of 22 December James had been out stealing fowls, but none were missing from Mr Dance's smallholding. The blood on his hands was easy to explain, as he had been killing chickens, and he would obviously wash it off at home. He had told Mrs Moody to say that he had not gone out until 8 p.m. The birds had probably been taken at 7 p.m. and sold to the Stanleys within the next thirty minutes or so. This was why he had burnt his boots, as they probably had telltale signs of the poaching on them. This poaching and transaction would also account for the money he had on him that evening. When James met Thomas Austin at 7.20 he did not have the price of a pint on him because the Stanleys had not yet bought the chickens. Later he had money to spend on his lady friend at the Flags, and he also told Mrs Moody he was expecting money from his slate club at the White Hart. This was a falsehood, but understandable in his wish to conceal the fact that he was about to get his money through poaching.

The only other evidence against his client was the sight of a tall man climbing Dance's fence, an allegation made by James Swain, who was walking his dog at the time. It must have been difficult on such a dark, wet night to be sure he had identified the man beyond all possible doubt.

Attenborough won the day. Thanks to his arguments and the Stanleys' deposition, on 6 February the jury was out for one hour before returning with a verdict of not guilty, and James was acquitted. As in the Reville murder case, the result startled the local community, who had been sure that William James would hang. Nobody else was ever arrested in connection with the murder.

14

'HOPING YOU WILL FORGIVE ME'

Newbury, 1891

In 1889 John Chamberlain married Annie Heath, and they settled at Warren Farm, Newbury. Every Sunday they attended the local Methodist chapel where Annie's 28-year-old brother Sidney, three years her senior, was the organist. Sidney was married with three children and lived near Newbury. To all outward appearances, they were a close-knit family.

On the evening of 15 January 1891, Annie told Sidney she would like to discuss some family business with him. John had just made his will, and had appointed Annie and Sidney joint executors. He was quite comfortably off, and as far as he knew there would be no more to it than the usual formalities. They sat talking in the sitting room for a while, then Sidney went to sit at the piano and started playing. As he did so, Annie told her husband she must have a word with her brother, and would he please leave them alone for a few minutes.

John went into the next room and heard what he assumed was normal conversation between them, followed by the sound of more piano music. Then suddenly the peace of the evening was shattered by a gunshot and a crashing discord on the piano – followed by an eerie silence. Horror-struck, John dashed back into the sitting room. Annie was standing in the middle of the room, holding a smoking long-barrel gun, while the body of her brother was slumped over the piano, covered in blood. He had been shot in the back of the head, and Annie had her finger on the trigger. John tried to force her to let go of the weapon, but she held on to it tenaciously and screamed. In the ensuing struggle, the gun went off again. Annie fell down dead with a bullet in her back.

Both shots had attracted the attention of Thomas Smith, a passing carter, who went to investigate and found John screaming. He calmed him down, then went for the police and a doctor. On arrival, Constable Holliday and Superintendent Bennett called for additional policemen to guard the property, then took possession of John's gun, which had been discharged in both barrels, and two spent cartridges. Dr William Clarke examined the bodies, but it was clear that both Annie and Sidney had died at once. The latter's head had been severely disfigured from a single shot at point-blank range, while the former had a wound slightly larger than a half-crown in the centre of her back, between the lower angles of the shoulder blades.

George Heath, their father, who lived at nearby Boames Farm, was informed immediately. He and his wife left at once for Warren Farm, slipping several times on the icy road. The police would not allow Mrs Heath inside the house as they thought the scene would be too harrowing for her. Meanwhile, John Chamberlain was frantic with grief, vowing that after it was all over, he would never set foot inside the farm again.

An inquest was held on 16 January at the ironically named Gun Inn. After he had opened proceedings, Dr Henry Watson, the coroner, and the jury walked to Warren Farm to see the scene for themselves. However, the building was double locked, and Superintendent Bennett had only one key. Nobody could find the second key, so one of the jurors had to break a window in order to let the police in to open the front door. After they had inspected the house, Dr Watson said that in his experience he had never seen a more sickening sight.

On returning to the Gun Inn to resume the inquest, he asked how Mrs Chamberlain could have shot herself in the back with a shotgun, which was larger than her. Alternatively, could the grieving husband have accidentally (or even deliberately) shot her himself? The neighbours had always known Annie as a cheerful, good-natured, conscientious lady, a regular churchgoer, and apparently sane. However, Dr Watson heard evidence that she was slightly mentally unhinged, and a suicide note had been found on the sideboard in the room of the farm. Addressed in her handwriting to her mother, it read:

> You have made our lives a misery to us all. This action I have done as a means of release from it. I can no longer keep from doing it. Hoping you will forgive me. Yours no longer, I remain.

George Heath, Annie's father, was astonished by the letter. He said that the family had always been very close, but he had thought his daughter's behaviour a little odd in recent weeks. The coroner asked what he could tell them as to the state of her mind. Mr Heath replied that there had been 'something that weighed on her nerves,' and that while he had never heard her uttering any threats, other members of the family had. He was sure she had been slightly unhinged, but on the previous day he asked John Chamberlain about it, and 'the answer did not seem quite satisfactory'. Although the family had seen a dark side to her which she kept concealed from the neighbours, they certainly had not expected her life to end in a tragedy of this magnitude.

John was next in the witness box. Still sobbing loudly, he found the situation impossible to explain. It was difficult to avoid the theory that there had been some secret between brother and sister which they did not want him to know about. Perhaps Sidney Heath knew something about his sister, or about the family in general, that she had no alternative but to silence him for ever. The other, admittedly rather uncharitable, possibility was that John had not been asked to leave the room, but could possibly have killed both victims himself and was putting on a very clever act.

After calming down a little, John told the court that after hearing the report from the gun, he ran into the room to find his wife standing in front of the fire, with the muzzle directed towards herself. (Considering the size of the gun, this sounded less than convincing.) He tried to remove the weapon from her grasp, and begged her to kiss him but she dashed past him and tried to go out through the door, while he was still trying to release the gun from her grip. She kept a firm grip on the muzzle, while he held on to the stock, and then it went off.

At this stage he broke down completely in hysterical sobs. After he had recovered, he went on to explain that the gun was never kept loaded in the house, and the cartridges were always kept separately. Annie had obviously had the gun loaded and this, coupled with the suicide note, indicated her intention to murder her brother, and possibly turn on her husband next. It did not look like an accident.

When asked if he and his wife had always lived happily together, he affirmed that this had been the case. Nevertheless, he agreed that Annie had 'acted rather strangely' on a few recent occasions. One night when they went to bed, she put her head at the bottom and her feet up on the pillow. She had also threatened to take her own life. When asked whether he thought the suicide note was definitely in her handwriting, he confirmed it. He also confirmed that he had checked the gun in the morning, and it was not loaded. He admitted that she had access to the ammunition, though he did not know whether she had ever been taught how to use a gun properly, as he was not aware that she had ever used it before. He kept the cartridges in a cupboard, and there had been some on the mantelpiece. That morning he had placed about twenty there to return to a friend from whom he had borrowed some. There had been no time for her to load the gun in the evening, so by the time her brother arrived at the farm it must have been already loaded and cocked.

When the coroner asked how Annie could have been shot in the back, John could not be positive. He could only say that she had been holding on to the barrel 'with deathly power', and admitted that he might have touched the trigger himself in the struggle. As she would have been quite capable of shooting him as deliberately as she had shot her brother, this was quite possible.

Dr Clarke told the court that Mrs Chamberlain had consulted him a few months before, after suffering a miscarriage. In his opinion she suffered from debility afterwards, and seemed to be 'of a highly nervous temperament', but beyond that there was nothing unusual in her condition. He agreed that her husband's account of how she was killed was possible, and there was no doubt in his mind that death was caused by a single gunshot wound accidentally inflicted during the struggle.

The coroner asked the jury whether they thought a post-mortem examination on Mrs Chamberlain was necessary. Philip Jackson, the foreman, said he was not satisfied they had heard the whole story. Dr Clarke said that a post-mortem would add nothing to what they knew already, and most of the jurors had decided for themselves that she would have shot herself anyway.

The coroner then mentioned the suicide note, and asked the witnesses whether they knew of any trouble in the family. They were unable to answer for certain, as it was apparent that there had been some ill-feeling. He could only conclude that there had been problems, 'and where is the family that there is not?'.

A few days later Sidney and Annie were buried together in the churchyard at Enborne, where several generations of their family had been buried before them. By this time there was some speculation about the role of John Chamberlain. It had emerged that his real name was Moses Belcher Whitehorn. His parents had been the licensees at the Blackbird Inn, Bagnor, near Newbury. They died when he was quite young and he was adopted by his mother's sister, the wife of Benjamin Chamberlain, a local dealer and farmer. On his death Benjamin had left Moses £3,000 on the condition that he changed his name to John Chamberlain. He had also been the beneficiary of his wife's will.

Dr Clarke said he had examined Annie about a fortnight before her death, and she appeared in good health at the time. Such an examination was necessary as her husband had taken out an insurance policy on her life for a large sum, the amount of which was never disclosed. Once this was known in the neighbourhood, there was speculation that her death might not have been the accident it appeared to be. After all, John Chamberlain was the only survivor from that fateful meeting on the night in question. What evidence, apart from his own testimony, was there that it had been Annie who shot her brother?

There were too many unanswered questions, and some of the jury suggested that as family troubles had been responsible for the act, some enquiry ought to be made into them. The coroner reminded them that all they had to enquire into was the cause of death, and on the evidence given there could be no doubt of that. After this the jury returned a verdict to the effect that Sidney Heath was shot by Mrs Chamberlain while the latter was 'suffering from temporary derangement', and that she was accidentally shot as her husband was trying to prevent her from attempting to commit suicide.

An application was made in the Queen's Bench Division for a new inquiry by the coroner into the cause of death on a person on whom he had already held an inquest, on the grounds that he had found the conclusion of the inquest 'insufficient and unsatisfactory'. This was a very rare instance, and only the third during the century. It was made under the Coroners' Act of 1887, which provided that when an inquest had been held by the coroner and by reason of the rejection of evidence or the insufficiency of the enquiry or otherwise it was felt necessary or desirable in the interests of justice that another inquiry should be held, the court could order another inquest. During a court hearing on 23 March, a representative of the coroner opposed the application, on the grounds that all the relevant points had been brought to the attention of the coroner and jury, and there was insufficient ground for demanding a second inquest.

John Chamberlain walked away a free man. If anybody actually believed there was any possibility that he had murdered his wife and managed to make it look like an accident, the authorities thought otherwise. As far as they were concerned, the only murder victim was Sidney Heath, and his sister's death had been a terrible accident. There was the theory that Annie was intent on suicide, and that the struggle was her attempt to provoke her husband into aiding and abetting her in the matter. John, however, remained true to his word, and never returned to the farmhouse.

15

FOUR SHOTS IN THE EVENING

Newbury, 1892

In the spring of 1892, twenty-four-year-old Ellis Wynn left Tonbridge, Kent, for Newbury to work in a jewellery shop. He had told everyone that he had independent means, and worked at the shop because he enjoyed doing so, rather than out of necessity. In a short while he would come into an inheritance from a relative, and then he planned to travel the world, before settling in Australia.

Only later did certain less palatable facts about his history come to light. He had been brought up in Kent, and as a small boy he used to keep snakes in his pocket. His parents were divorced; his father had attempted to murder his mother by cutting her throat, and had been sentenced to twenty years in prison. This unhappy family background cast a shadow from which he would never be totally free during his short life.

Soon after arriving at Newbury, Wynn became friendly with Edith Stevens, a young woman who worked in a drapery shop nearby in Market Place, owned by Alfred Jackson, the town mayor. A few weeks later he announced that he was about to set out on his travels, and would be stopping first at Naples. In May 1892 he left Newbury for a few days, then returned to see Stevens.

They spent Sunday 15 May together walking around Savernake Forest in Wiltshire, and it was then that Edith began to see a disturbing new side to her friend. While they were together Wynn produced a revolver from his pocket and threatened to kill himself. Calmly she took it from his hand, and also retrieved thirty-two cartridges from his pocket. He apologised for his behaviour and she handed everything back, but not before extracting from him a promise that he would never threaten to do anything so silly again.

Returning from their day out, they spent some time with friends in Craven Road, and decided to spend the night there. After the women had retired to bed, Wynn stayed up later talking to his friend, Francis Andrews. He complained of severe headaches and reiterated his intention to shoot himself. The relative from whom he had been expecting a large inheritance had cut him off without a penny, and contrary to what he had been telling everybody, he had no money of his own and was deep in debt. An alarmed Andrews searched Wynn's coat pockets once his back was turned, and found the revolver with the cartridges, which he locked away overnight.

On 16 May Edith Stevens went to her work as usual, having arranged to meet Wynn later. He seemed more his old self again, and spent part of the day going round Newbury saying goodbye to his friends, as he was about to set off on his travels. He told Andrews he felt much more settled, and asked if he could have the revolver back as he wanted to return it to the friend in Reading from whom he had borrowed it. Reassured that matters had somehow resolved themselves and that Wynn was no longer suicidal, Andrews gave it back.

That evening, Wynn met Stevens after she had finished her work for the day. They walked arm-in-arm through the town, with one of Edith's colleagues, Lizzie Pecover, accompanying them. She left them at the junction of Enborne Road and walked home, as they continued down the lane leading to Enborne Gate Farm.

Darkness had fallen by 10 p.m. just as a shepherd, John Quelch, heard three shots, then a pause followed by a fourth. Sergeant Edmund Holding, patrolling the town centre, heard likewise, and walked in the direction of the farm to investigate. He and Quelch arrived at the scene at about the same time. There they found two bodies in a pool of blood: Wynn had shot Stevens once in the back and twice in the head, then placed the weapon in his mouth and pulled the trigger. He was still clutching the revolver in his right hand.

An inquest was held the next day on the farm, and doctors performed a post-mortem. The jury inspected the bodies as Dr William Clarke gave evidence. There was a great deal of blood around the face of Miss Stevens, he said, especially around the nose and mouth, with a hole in the skull on the left side, on the top of the head, from which the brain was protruding. Her jaw was completely shattered, suggesting that the gun had been fired into her open mouth. A bullet was lodged in the brain, and had fractured the skull just above the right ear.

As for the body of Mr Wynn, the doctor said the mouth showed signs of scorching, and he had no doubt that the weapon was fired directly into the mouth. The bullet had gone through the roof of his mouth, the centre and base of the skull, the middle of the brain, and out of the top of the head. Death must have been instantaneous.

The coroner made a few remarks on the relative ease of obtaining firearms, regretting that they could readily be purchased for a few shillings. Evidence was offered as to the likelihood that Wynn was mentally unbalanced, but the coroner reminded the jury that it was their duty to establish how the young couple had died,

Market Place, Newbury.
(© Brian Robert Marshall)

and not to indulge in speculation. They duly returned a verdict that Wynn murdered Miss Stevens, and then took his own life.

The bodies were taken to a mortuary at the back of the Corn Exchange. Wynn lay there for several days while arguments ensued as to who was responsible for meeting the costs of his burial. In his pocket was found a gold watch, but after enquiries were made it turned out that he had borrowed it from a friend, who wanted it back, so it could not be sold to defray funeral expenses. Eventually some of his acquaintances held a collection, so his body could be removed from the mortuary at midnight and taken to the cemetery chapel in a plain elm coffin with black handles. He was buried without ceremony at dawn and the grave was immediately filled in, without any marker being left at the spot. Edith Stevens made her last journey by train to her home town of Watford, where she received a Christian burial.

The spot where the bodies had been discovered became a site of morbid interest. During the weeks after the murder many people visited the site, marked by a cross cut in the turf at the side of the road.

16

'IS IT FOR EVER, DEAR HEART?'

Reading, 1896

Charles Thomas Wooldridge grew up in East Garston on the Lambourn Downs. As a young man he joined the army, and, appropriately for someone who had grown up with and always loved horses, he joined the Royal Horse Guards. From time to time he was on guard duty at Windsor Castle.

On 9 October 1894 he married Laura Ellen Glendell, a native of Bath, at St Martin's Church, Kentish Town. At the time he was aged twenty-eight and she was twenty-one. His commanding officer had refused him permission to marry, so they held the ceremony in secret. For a while they settled at 28 Waldington Street, London, then they moved to Windsor. Nell, as Laura she was called by her family, worked as an assistant to the postmistress in the office at High Street, Eton, where she was known by her maiden name.

From the start it was a troubled union. Husband and wife quarrelled regularly, he drank too much, and she carried on with other men behind his back. Within a few months they were living apart most of the time, and the marriage was dead in all but name. Even so, Charles bitterly resented Nell's infidelities. He was extremely possessive, but if she had been faithful to him, he would probably have made more of an effort to mend their relationship.

At the age of thirty, during the early spring 1896, Charles was posted to London. He was stationed at Hyde Park Barracks for guard duty at Buckingham Palace, when news reached him of his wife's latest infidelities, almost certainly through the other soldiers' gossip. Extremely upset, he decided to go absent without leave in order to try and sort matters out at home. In spite of their difficulties he was still devoted to her, and had probably convinced himself that he could not live without her. He made up his mind that if he could not have her, then he would ensure that no other man ever would.

On 27 March Charles returned to Nell's house at 21 Alma Terrace, Clewer. His niece, Alice Cox, had been living with her since 11 January. At the door Nell asked him angrily what he wanted. He said he had come to see her, and they went into another room where they could talk in private. Half an hour later Alice heard Nell crying, and opened the door to find her lying on the floor with her nose bleeding. When she asked what the matter was, Nell said Charles had hit her. 'Oh, what have I done?' exclaimed Wooldridge. 'Why did you try my temper so, Nell?'

Nell told Alice to put on her hat and fetch a friend from the cavalry barracks. Alice went out as directed but did not find him. By the time she had returned Charles was gone. Nell was standing outside the front door, and while she was talking to Alice, Wooldridge returned, handed Nell a note, and bid her goodnight. He then asked her if she would object to Miss Cox coming with him for a short walk, and she reluctantly agreed. As he and his niece strolled along the road, he said how sorry he was for having struck his wife, hoped she would forgive him, and then left.

Although he blamed himself for losing his temper, Charles thought Nell's behaviour had been extremely provocative. As he returned to barracks, he was under the impression that she had promised to come and see him there on 29 March, but if she ever agreed to do so, she probably had no intention of keeping her word, for she never turned up. Trooper James Jobson, of the Royal Horse Guards, was on sentry duty that day at the main gate at Hyde Park Barracks. Wooldridge asked him to keep an eye out for his wife, as he was not allowed to do so himself. When she did not appear, he said he would have to go to Windsor, and would return to barracks by the last train. Ominously, he told Jobson, 'I must go, for I am going to do some damage.'

Again without seeking permission, Wooldridge slipped away and boarded a train to Windsor. This, he had almost certainly decided, would be their last chance at reconciliation. That Sunday evening, at about 9 p.m., he was back at 21 Alma Street. When Alice heard a knock at the door she thought it was their lodger. She opened up to let him in and Charles told her he had some papers for his wife to sign. Sitting down at the table, he began to write on a document, to which was affixed a 6d stamp. The message, which was followed by his signature, read:

> I hereby promise never to come near, or see, or in any way to molest, Laura Ellen Glendell. This is my oath, taken in front of a witness.

Miss Cox had been sitting in the parlour with Nell, who asked her to fetch her hat and jacket. While Alice went to get them, husband and wife went out of the front door towards an iron wicket gate separating the forecourt from the street. She goaded him, saying he was an inadequate husband, and at this any determination Charles might have had to keep calm vanished. In a blind fury he took a razor from his pocket and lunged at her. She screamed and ran into the middle of the road, where he seized her and drew the weapon across her throat.

Shortly afterwards Constable Miles, his attention attracted by the screams, reached the scene and informed his immediate superior, Superintendent Read of the Berkshire Constabulary. They summoned medical aid, and the lifeless body of Mrs Wooldridge was carried into the house. Meanwhile a crowd of horrified neighbours, curious to see what had happened, was gathering around until the police asked them to disperse.

By this time, Wooldridge had met Constable Foster and told him that he had attacked his wife, assuring him that she was dead but she deserved it because she had been 'carrying on a fine game, as she had some lawyer in tow'. If he had not left the razor behind, he added, he would have killed himself too. He was handed over to Superintendent Armour, and remained in custody overnight.

A few hours before the murder, Nell had written a letter to her husband's commanding officer. As she had no chance to send it, it was found in a box of papers at the house in Alma Street a few days later, and published in full in the press that week. It read:

> Pardon me troubling you: I would not do so if I could help it. I write to tell you about Charles Wooldridge. He came down about a fortnight ago and behaved in a most strange manner, and had some sort of fit. Friday he came down in the evening and we disagreed, and he struck me as violently as he could in the face, blackening my left eye and causing my cheek to swell and become discoloured, and it is most painful now. I told him I should complain to his officer about him, and he promised he would sign a paper, stating that he would never come near me again. May I ask you to make him do this and send me, as I feel far from safe? He might come again and repeat the treatment, and as I am in business at Windsor I should lose my situation if I prosecuted him, and, of course, he knows that. I had to tell my employer this morning that I had fallen downstairs and so disfigured myself. I do not write this to get Wooldridge punished, I want him to sign that paper so I may have a safeguard against his coming. May I implore you never to let him come down here again? If you would grant me an interview I could explain everything to you which I cannot do by writing. Please allow me to see you. I could come on Friday next if this would suit, as it is a holiday. If you reply to this letter, kindly address to Miss Glendell at the above address.

Also in the box was the couple's marriage certificate, and a long, undated letter from Charles, written from his Albany Street address, which likewise found its way into the hands of the press. In it he claimed that Nell had no need to get the police or anybody else to look after her house, as he promised he would never molest her and she would be perfectly safe. He assured her that he would never speak to another woman as long as he lived, begged her not to get married again, or write to his colonel, as it would do him a great deal of harm, and implored her not to bring any legal action against him:

Agree to this, my dear, for me to stay away from you while I am in the army, and when I have finished my time then come and join you, dear. Will you agree to that, because I have not done you any harm, dearie? I am very sorry for what I have done, dear. I wish you could forgive me, darling; but I have brought it on myself, so I must suffer for it, if you don't forgive me, darling ... Don't forget to send me a photo of your darling face, then I can see you sometimes. I shall have to kiss your photo, dear, and know it's my dear wife, and that's been good and kind to me, and I have not served her as I ought, and how I am cast out. Is it for ever, dear heart? Will my wife have a little pity on me, and say I shall be here if I am a good boy when I have finished my soldiering? I hope you will ...

Yet another letter found in the front room at Alma Terrace, on the mantelpiece, was written from Nell to her father. It was a request for him to help her find another position, if possible at a district post office, as she had no chance of promotion if she stayed where she was. As the letter to the commanding officer suggested, she was anxious that any scandal would make her employers take a dim view of the situation.

Above left: *Charles Wooldridge. (*Lloyds Weekly Newspaper*)*

Above right: *Nell Wooldridge. (*Lloyds Weekly Newspaper*)*

Alma Terrace, Clewer, Windsor. (Lloyds Weekly Newspaper)

On the morning of Monday 30 March, Charles Wooldridge was removed from his cell to the superintendent's office, taken before Mr E.B. Foster, a Berkshire magistrate, and remanded in custody until Saturday 4 April, when he would be brought before the Berkshire Petty Sessions. That afternoon he travelled by train to Reading. On the journey he expressed contrition to his escort for the offence, saying he was sorry 'the poor thing' was dead, and that he was willing to die himself.

On 31 March, an inquest was held at the Elephant and Castle, Oxford Road, Windsor by the Berkshire coroner, William Weedon. Alice Cox appeared as a witness, and told the court that Mr and Mrs Wooldridge had quarrelled last Monday week, 23 March, though she was not there when the disagreement took place. Her uncle had left the premises on Tuesday morning and returned on Friday 27 March, at about 7 p.m.

The next witness was Frederick William Davis, a tailor who lived at Arthur Road. He said that on the Sunday night at about 9.10 he heard a noise and screaming outside the house. As he went out to investigate, he saw a man running past. Another man, glancing at him, remarked, 'There he goes; he has done something to her up there.' The man running past stopped briefly and turned, then continued running.

Davis then saw a woman's body in the road, and he put his hand under her head to keep it up. Blood was coming from her throat, and his hands were immediately covered as well. Although he spoke to her, asking her who had done it, she seemed to take no notice, as 'she was too far gone'. A young woman, whom he assumed to be Miss Cox, came out of the house, and mentioned her by name. He noticed that as the moon shone into the dying woman's eyes, he 'could see they were changing'.

Next, Constable John Foster, of the Windsor police, said he was in Peascod Street that night. At about 9.20 p.m. Wooldridge walked up to him, saying, 'Take me, I've killed my wife.' He cautioned Wooldridge to be careful what he was saying, but the latter merely repeated himself, adding that he had cut his wife's throat with a razor and she was dead. As Foster took him to the station Charles showed him his hands, which were covered with blood.

Nell was buried on 1 April at St Andrew's Church, Clewer. Wreaths were sent by her parents, her friends, and the *Windsor Telegraph* messengers.

On 4 April Charles appeared before the Berkshire Petty Sessions at Windsor Guildhall, charged with murder. Evidence was given again by Alice Cox, who said that Nell told her she had sent her husband a document to sign 'to give her her release', with a clause binding him not to come near her again. While she was fetching Nell's hat and jacket, she heard screaming. She ran downstairs to find Charles in the road leaning over Nell's prostrate body. He said, 'No, no, I'll give myself up.' She could not make out his face, but recognised him by the sound of his voice. Under cross-examination she said that at about the end of February Mrs Wooldridge had once brought a Robert Harvey, a soldier with two stripes upon his arm, back to the house with her, and he had stayed from about 7 to 9.30 p.m. When he left the house, she noticed him shake hands with Nell, but did not kiss her. He was the only soldier, with the exception of the accused, that she had ever seen in the place.

Charles Wooldridge pleaded not guilty. His lawyer tried to have the charge reduced to manslaughter on the grounds of provocation, alleging in mitigation that Trooper Harvey 'had caused jealousy between the prisoner and his wife.' The bench decided otherwise, and he was committed to Reading Assizes.

The trial began on 25 June before Mr Justice Hawkins, with Charles Wooldridge still pleading not guilty to a charge of murder. In addition to repeating the evidence she had previously given with regard to the prisoner's visits to his wife, Alice Cox said that he had always been very fond of her. Mrs Wooldridge had once told Alice, 'I think my husband is mad,' and she had been very cold towards her husband for some time. George Atkins of the Royal Horse Guards said that the razor with which the deed was committed was his property, and he had lent it to the prisoner eleven days before the murder. Among other witnesses called were James Jobson, the sentry, who spoke again of having kept a watch out for Mrs Wooldridge at Hyde Park on 29 March but in vain, Constable Foster, and Dr Wyborn, who gave evidence as to the extent of Mrs Wooldridge's wounds.

The title page from The Ballad of Reading Gaol, by C33, alias Oscar Wilde, by Frank Masereel, published 1924.

A woodcut from The Ballad of Reading Gaol, showing prisoners exercising in the yard.

For the defence, Mr Walsh submitted that they would be justified in reducing the charge to one of manslaughter. There was undoubtedly provocation, and he asked the jury to believe that the prisoner killed his wife in a fit of frenzy. Nevertheless, Charles was found guilty of murder, but with a recommendation to mercy. Mr Justice Hawkins sentenced Wooldridge to death, and the Home Secretary refused to issue a reprieve.

Wooldridge accepted his fate calmly, saying that he deserved it, and was sent to Reading Gaol to await execution. In a conversation with the chaplain, Revd M.T. Friend, he expressed his sorrow for having taken away his wife's life, and he hoped he would meet her in heaven. He spent his last few weeks fully resigned to his fate.

While at Reading Gaol, an even more famous prisoner was serving a two-year sentence there. In May 1895 Oscar Wilde had been imprisoned for homosexuality, following his loss of a libel action. The two men never met, but as Wooldridge was the only man to be executed at Reading Gaol during this time, the poet and playwright was morbidly fascinated by the impending fate of the young soldier, whom he sometimes saw from a distance in the exercise yard. After his release in 1897, Wilde spent the remaining three years of his life in France and wrote a lengthy epic poem *The Ballad of*

Reading Gaol – the only piece of literature he wrote after his release from prison – while staying in a small hotel near Dieppe. As Wilde's name was considered too notorious for the front cover of any new publication, it appeared in 1898 under the pseudonym C33 (building C, floor 3, cell 3), with a dedication to CTW. As the last line of the first verse shows, it made up in atmosphere for what it occasionally lacked in accuracy:

> He did not wear his scarlet coat,
> For blood and wine are red,
> And blood and wine were on his hands
> When they found him with the dead,
> The poor dead woman whom he loved,
> And murdered in her bed.

While he was awaiting execution, Wooldridge hoped that his father would pay him a final visit. The elder man came to Reading to see his son, but on his arrival he was so overwhelmed with grief that he was unable to do so, and left without saying a final farewell.

Despite regular examinations by the prison doctor, Dr Maurice, Wooldridge seemed in good health and spirits, and ate hearty meals. On the morning of 7 July, after a good breakfast and last meetings with the prison governor and chief warder, he walked to the scaffold, 'with that firmness which had characterised his demeanour throughout.'

17

THE NOTORIOUS
MRS DYER

Reading, 1896

Baby farmers commonly occur in the annals of nineteenth-century crime in Britain. These women placed advertisements in newspapers, offering to adopt babies from mothers who had conceived outside of wedlock and found the infants 'inconvenient', for a small fee, or not so small, depending on their means. It appeared to be a useful facility in an age when middle-class single mothers were regarded as having put themselves outside respectable society. They would rarely if ever be able to check on the progress of their children, as the so-called carers would place obstacles in their way, and the mothers would be too ashamed to go to the police. Unknown to the mothers, these babies were almost always killed soon after being handed over, either through neglect, drowning or poison. Eight baby farmers were hanged in Britain for murder between 1870 and 1909, and several others charged with the same offence were fortunate to escape the death sentence.

As far as records show, Mrs Amelia Dyer was probably the most prolific baby farming murderer of her age. Much of her early life is shrouded in mystery and conflicting information. According to various sources, Amelia Hobley was born in 1829, 1838 or 1839 (probably the latter), the youngest of five children. Her father, Samuel Hobley, was a cordwainer, or master shoemaker, and she was brought up near Bristol. She had a good education and a happy childhood until she was about eleven, when her mother was sent to an asylum and later died from some unspecified disease. At fourteen she left home to live with an aunt, and was later apprenticed to a corset maker.

In 1861 Amelia married a widower, George Thomas, about thirty-four years her senior. Two years later she took up a nursing position at Bristol Royal Infirmary, but had to give it up within a year when she became pregnant with her first daughter,

Ellen. George died in 1869, and in 1872 she married William Dyer, a labourer, six years her junior. Their first child, Mary Ann (always known as Polly), was born in 1873, and their second, William Samuel, in 1876. Amelia would later claim that she had given birth to thirteen children, most of whom died in infancy. In view of subsequent events, it was possible that very few of these were actually her biological children. Two weeks after her death in 1896, the *Weekly Dispatch* carried a signed statement by Polly, in which she revealed that just before her marriage she was told by her mother that her real parents were a farmer and his wife, relations on her father's side.

Mrs Dyer soon found a more lucrative way of earning a living. At first she used her home to provide lodgings for young women who were expecting outside of marriage. The appeal of this soon waned, especially once she realised there was considerable money to be made from advertising to adopt or nurse babies in return for a substantial one-off payment and plenty of clothing for the infant. After placing advertisements in local newspapers, desperate young women would arrange to meet her, and she assured them she was a respectable married lady who could give the children a steady, loving home. The mothers would assume that their baby son or daughter was in good hands; most of them were glad to relieve themselves of the living proof of their 'indiscretion' and start again, though some might look forward to visiting the children again before long and perhaps reclaim them, financial and other considerations permitting. Few, if any, would ever see their offspring again. At least one who did found it was in the heartbreaking circumstances of having to identify their child on a mortuary slab.

By using several aliases in her advertisements in which she asked for children to

adopt, and by constantly changing her address in the Bristol area, Amelia Dyer pocketed many a fee, callously disposed of several small babies, and then sold the clothes given her by the mother as well. By 1879 a doctor, suspicious after being called in to certify so many deaths of children in her care, called the police. As a result of the ensuing investigation Amelia swallowed two bottles of laudanum, which could have proved fatal, but only succeeded in making herself extremely sick. When charged at Bristol with attempted suicide and gross negligence, resulting in

Amelia Dyer.

the deaths of at least two and possibly four or more children in her care, she was sentenced to six months' imprisonment with hard labour in Shepton Mallet Gaol, an experience which came close to destroying her mental reason.

For the rest of her life, Mrs Dyer pursued the baby farming 'business' sporadically, and moved with increasing regularity in order to keep one step ahead of the police. Realising that to involve doctors in issuing death certificates for babies in her care was unwise, she disposed of the bodies herself instead. It was easy enough to suffocate one and abandon it in the middle of a city, or wrap it in linen and a parcel, add a brick and throw it in the river. Lest suspicious parents and police might show too much interest in her, she and her family continued to move regularly. Sometimes they would enter a new house on a Saturday and be out again by the following Tuesday. The effect on her husband and children can be imagined. For the youngsters it was most unsettling, while William became increasingly withdrawn and taciturn, though he seemed prepared to tolerate his wife's obnoxious trade as long as it brought in money.

One middle-class mother who gave her baby up for adoption handed over £80 for being relieved of her tiny burden, a sum equivalent to at least three years' wages for the average labourer. Nevertheless, arguments between husband and wife increased, as did the number of house moves, and Polly resented being ordered to lie to her father about her mother's movements and absences. At the time of the 1891 census Mrs Dyer was being pursued by a former governess and her husband, who had given birth outside wedlock and had handed the baby over. The child's father, having originally

Shepton Mallet Gaol. (Courtesy of Nicola Sly)

refused to marry her, changed his mind and they decided they wanted their child back. Although ultimately unsuccessful, they were so persistent that Mrs Dyer temporarily disappeared, and Mr Dyer told the census official that he was a widower. Shortly after, he walked out on her.

Over the years, Amelia spent short periods of time in asylums for mental instability and efforts to take her own life. In November 1891 she was admitted to Gloucester Asylum for attempting to cut her throat, but she was discharged within a month. In December 1893 she was in Wells Asylum after trying to drown herself, but again only stayed three or four weeks.

Between March and April 1895 she was in the Bristol workhouse, and again that July. One month later she was back in Gloucester Asylum. Later, the police discovered an interesting pattern; her confinements in the asylums corresponded with times when inquiries were being made regarding children who had been placed in her care. During one twelve-month period she was believed to have been living at Eastville as Mrs Smith, at Ashley as Mrs Waltham, at Fishponds and even at Notting Hill in London, as well as at Caversham, accompanied by her daughter and son-in-law, Polly and Arthur Palmer, and a friend and associate, Jane Smith. The latter, aged about seventy, was a widow whose children had died, and whom she had met in one of the workhouses. A kindly yet naïve soul who adored children, Jane had befriended Mrs Dyer and was only too keen to return to the outside world. She fondly imagined that both women would be the best of friends, almost like sisters, and that she would be able to help look after the young children.

By the time Mrs Dyer moved to Kensington Road, Reading, the long arm of the law was beginning to catch up with her. Had she decided to stop while she was still ahead, she might have saved herself. But she had not realised that her extraordinary combination of cunning and good fortune was about to come to a sudden end.

In January 1896 Evelina Marmon, a barmaid of twenty-five, gave birth to a daughter, Doris, in a Cheltenham boarding-house, and placed an advertisement in the *Bristol Times & Mirror*, asking for a respectable woman to take a young child. She planned to return to work, and reclaim her child at some later stage when it would be convenient. By coincidence her notice appeared next to one reading, 'Married couple with no family would adopt healthy child, nice country home. Terms, £10.' Evelina answered the advertisement, and a few days later had a reply from a 'Mrs Harding', saying how glad she would be to have a dear little baby girl to bring up and call her own. The letter described her family as 'plain homely people, in fairly good circumstances', saying she and her husband were very fond of children. As she had no child of her own, Evelina's daughter would 'have a good home and a mother's love'.

When Evelina went to visit Mrs Harding, she was surprised to be met by an elderly, stocky woman, although she seemed very affectionate towards little Doris. The young mother wanted to pay a weekly fee for her daughter's care, which she felt would be more affordable, but was told the one-off payment of £10 was non-negotiable, and, being desperate, she was in no position to argue. Distressed at having to give up the child, she handed over her daughter, the cash, and a box of clothes. She then accompanied Mrs Dyer to Cheltenham station, and then to Gloucester, before returning to her lodgings, sad and alone but buoyed up by the thought that one day she would be reunited with little Doris, whom she had been told was going to Reading. A few days later she received a short, friendly letter saying that all was well.

In fact, Mrs Dyer had not returned to Reading at all, but had travelled to Mayo Road, Willesden, London, where Polly and her husband Arthur were staying. She took some white edging tape, wound it twice around the baby's neck and knotted it tightly. Mother and daughter then wrapped the body in a napkin, keeping some of the clothes and putting others aside to take to the pawnbroker. On the following day another child, Harry Simmons, the son of a ladies' maid from Ealing, was taken to Mayo Road to be looked after. As Mrs Dyer and Polly had run out of edging tape, the thrifty pair removed the piece from around Doris's neck so they could use it to strangle the little boy. Both bodies were bundled ruthlessly into a carpet bag, with bricks to weigh them down. Mrs Dyer then returned to Reading, and at a secluded spot near a weir at Caversham with which she had long been familiar, she forced the bag through the railings and into the river.

Earlier that week, on 30 March, a bargeman on the Thames at Reading had retrieved a curious-looking package from the river. When he discovered to his horror that it contained tiny human limbs, he handed it to the Reading Borough Police, who identified the corpse as that of Helena Fry. Mary Fry, a domestic servant in Bristol, had handed her over to Mrs Dyer at Bristol Temple Meads station on 5 March. That evening the latter returned home with the already dead infant in a brown parcel, and placed it in a cupboard in the back of the kitchen. Over the next few days the smell became unbearable, though it was not for another twenty-five days that she washed the stinking cupboard out thoroughly, removed the package and threw it in the river. As she did not weight it properly, it never sank to the bottom.

River Thames, Reading, looking downstream towards Thames Valley Park. (© Andrew Smith).

Constable Anderson was placed in charge of the case, and he identified a label on the wrapping marked from Temple Meads station. Further analysis revealed a barely legible name which looked like 'Mrs Thomas', and an address. This proved enough to connect it with Mrs Dyer, but the police had no firm evidence that she was involved. Anderson and Sergeant James therefore placed her home in Reading under discreet surveillance, in the knowledge that she would abscond and go elsewhere if she knew she was being watched. Next they found a young woman to use as a decoy, hoping to arrange a meeting with Dyer at which she could pretend to ask her to adopt another baby.

When Mrs Dyer opened the door on 3 April to what she assumed was another trusting client, she found several policemen outside. They carried out a thorough search of her home, and although they found no human remains, there was an appalling stench of decomposition in the house, the result of her storage of the parcel containing Helena Fry. Also discovered were a roll of edging tape, telegrams discussing adoption arrangements, pawn tickets for children's clothing, letters from mothers wanting to know about their babies' welfare, and notes suggesting that she was planning a move to Somerset. It was calculated that in the previous few months, at least twenty children had been placed in the care of 'Mrs Thomas'.

Mrs Dyer, alias Thomas, alias Harding, of Kensington Road, Reading, was arrested on 4 April and charged with the murder of Helena Fry. Arthur Palmer, who lived at Mayo Road, was arrested as an accessory. During the next few days the Thames was dragged on the instructions of Superintendent Tewsley, and another six bodies in carpet bags were discovered. Among them were those of Doris Marmon and Harry Simmons, destined to be the last of her many victims. They were found similarly strangled which, as the murderess later told the police, was how they could tell these were her victims. Eleven days after she had handed her daughter to Mrs Dyer, Evelina Marmon, whose name had been found in some of the paperwork at the house, was called to identify the remains of her daughter. When she was told by the police of her daughter's fate, she collapsed with shock.

On 11 April Mrs Dyer made her first appearance before Reading Magistrates Court, charged with 'having on or about March 20th in the Parish of St Mary, Reading, feloniously killed and murdered a female child unknown'. Arthur Palmer was also charged with being 'an accessory after the fact', as on 30 March he knowingly concealed the murder of the child with intent to enable Mrs Dyer 'to elude the pursuit of justice'. As the identity of the victim was unknown, and as various other matters had since come to the knowledge of the police, in particular the discovery of more victims, the case was then adjourned until the following week.

That same evening, 11 April, an inquest was held at the St Giles Coffee House, Reading, by the coroner, William Weedon, into the deaths of Doris Marmon and Harry Simmons. Among the witnesses was Evelina Marmon, who confirmed that the female infant in the mortuary was her daughter. When she said that 'Mrs Harding' had promised to give her daughter a happy home, the coroner remarked reproachfully, 'All for £10, an easy way of getting rid of a child. I don't know how you could expect it to be done.'

At her second court appearance on 18 April, Mrs Dyer was charged with the murders of Helena Fry, Doris Marmon and Harry Simmons, and Palmer with being an accessory. Evelina Marmon was in court as a witness, and she produced the letter she had received from Mrs Dyer before handing Doris over.

On 24 April Mrs Dyer had a meeting in her cell with the solicitor's managing clerk and a shorthand writer. She gave them some confidential notes she had made about the case, among which was a letter of confession. Four days later it appeared on the front page of the *Daily Courier*. Addressed, 'Sir', presumably her solicitor, she admitted there was no chance of her life being saved, 'unless you plead upon the cause of insanity,' in view of her having been an inmate at various asylums in the past, her suicide attempts, and her mother's death in an asylum at the age of forty-five. The Home Office was horrified that the letter should have been made public, and an inquiry was launched to investigate the breach in security procedures at Reading Gaol.

At a third appearance by Mrs Dyer and Palmer on 25 April, the police produced witnesses to testify that children had appeared at the addresses at Kensington Road, Piggotts Road, and Elm Villas, Lower Caversham. None of them were ever seen again. Charles Culham, a carriage cleaner, of Mayo Road, Willesden, told how Mrs Dyer had paid in advance for her daughter and son-in-law to lodge at his house. He said he had had a fireplace moved, and some surplus bricks were stacked behind the house, some of which he used to support a rabbit hutch and a clothes post for his wife's washing line. A detective produced the bricks used to weight some of the bodies found in the driver, and Culham confirmed that they had come from his house. The coroner's court recorded a verdict of wilful murder on the first three bodies.

Mrs Dyer appeared for the last time before Reading magistrates on 2 May, by which time a seventh body, that of a baby boy, had been retrieved from the river. At her daughter's insistence, this time she had a solicitor and two barristers representing her. Prosecuting on behalf of the Treasury, Mr Justice A.T. Lawrence told the court he had come to the conclusion that there was insufficient evidence with which to charge Palmer, and he was released from custody. The court was told of Dyer's confession, written while in custody on 16 April, exonerating her son-in-law and daughter. Addressed to the Superintendent of Police, and reproduced here verbatim, it read:

Will you kindly grant me the favour of presenting this to the magistrates on Satturday the 18th instant. I have made this statement now, for I may not have the opportunity then. I must relieve my mind. I do know and I feel my days are numbered on this earth but I do feel it is an awful thing drawing innocent people into trouble. I do know I shall have to answer before my Maker in Heaven for the awful crimes I have committed but as God Almighty is my judge in Heaven as on Earth neither my daughter Mary Ann Palmer nor her husband Alfred Ernest Palmer I do most solemnly declare neither of them had any thing at all to do with it, they never knew I contemplated doing such a wicked thing until it was too late I am speaking the truth and nothing but the truth as I hope to be forgiven, I myself and I alone must stand before my Maker in Heaven to give a answer for it all witnes my hand Amelia Dyer.

As the clerk finished reading, Mrs Dyer showed her first sign of emotion. When her daughter's name was mentioned, she buried her head in her hands and wept.

Her counsel, Mr Kapadia, said her sanity was in doubt, and she had written the letter while of unsound mind. The Bench rejected his application, saying that the prisoner's mental state would be determined by a judge and jury, and she was committed for trial at the Old Bailey.

Having been released, Arthur Palmer was arrested a second time. On 4 May, at Devonport, Alfred Ernest Palmer, alias Alfred Parsons, alias Alfred Potson, was charged with wilfully abandoning a child, Queenie Baker, while he and his wife were staying at Gloucester Cottages, Devonport, on or around 17 May 1895. They were at the premises for about a week, during which time it was noticed they received a large number of parcels. When they left, they abandoned Queenie, aged nearly four, in the street. When found, she was taken to the police station, and subsequently adopted by a lady in Devonport. Appearing before the town magistrates, Palmer pleaded guilty and was sentenced to three months' hard labour.

Amelia Dyer being mobbed on her way to Reading Magistrates Court, 2 May 1896.
(Weekly Dispatch)

Mr Justice A.T. Lawrence. (Courtesy of Nicola Sly)

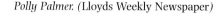

Polly Palmer. (Lloyds Weekly Newspaper)

Amelia Dyer was charged with the murders of Doris Marmon and Harry Simmons. Her trial under Mr Justice Hawkins opened on 21 May, and lasted two days. She offered a defence of insanity, and Mr Kapadia made much of the fact that she was 'unaccountable for her actions' at the time of the killings, as well as her committals to the asylums. The prosecution argued that she had arranged to be committed merely to try and avoid suspicion, as it always happened at times when she was concerned her crimes might have been exposed. According to evidence from witnesses, and various receipts, letters and other paperwork found in her house, many more children had probably met the same fate, and the exact number would never be known.

Evidence was given by Evelina Marmon, and by Mary Ann Beattie from Mayo Road, who had seen Mrs Dyer carrying a carpet bag which probably contained Doris Marmon. Polly Palmer was also called as a main witness against her mother, and it was noticed that she looked harassed and pale. Her answers were not always satisfactory. When asked to explain how the items of clothing that had belonged to Doris Marmon and Harry Simmonds had ended up at her house, she told the court her mother had brought them, saying they had been made for Polly's own 'nurse child', Harold,[1] for whom she had received an adoption fee of £12. When the judge asked her if she really wanted to adopt a child, she answered, 'yes'. 'Then why not take it without any money?' She could not answer. With some reluctance she said her mother had called Harry 'a little devil' as he was fretful, shook him, and said she 'shouldn't keep it'.

Under cross-examination by Mr Kapadia, Polly said her mother had been confined in the asylums and often suffered from delusions. On the second day of the trial, she told of the many children her mother had taken into care during the years, and of the many changes of address. When asked how many children her mother had at her different residences, she could not say.

Further evidence was given Mr and Mrs Culham, the prison staff, and her assistant Jane Smith[2]. Over the months, Mrs Smith had become increasingly disturbed at Mrs Dyer's treatment of some of the babies in her care, in particular her impatience with any who were teething or fretful for any reason. She was puzzled to come down in the mornings and find that the baby she had said goodnight to the previous evening was no longer there. When she was told that the mother had collected it, she wondered why the clothes had not gone as well. Further questions only led to ill-tempered exchanges, and at one stage early in 1896 Jane walked out to return to the workhouse at Reading. Mrs Dyer had guessed where she was, and went there to invite her back, promising she would be kinder in future. Yet by the time of the trial, Mrs Smith had no qualms of conscience about testifying to some of the more suspicious movements. Most damning of all was her evidence that a brick which she had used to rest her flat iron on in the house was the same one later found in one of the carpet bags hauled out from the Thames.

Mr Kapadia's efforts to prove Mrs Dyer's insanity were in vain. Dr Frederick Logan of Bristol, who had committed her to an asylum in 1894, told the court that she was violent, suffered from delusions, and had told him she heard voices and birds in her head, telling her to kill herself. Nevertheless, two specialists who had examined her more recently were called by the prosecution, and said that in their opinion she was perfectly sane at the time the last babies were killed.

The jury only took five minutes to find her guilty of murder. Donning the black cap, Mr Justice Hawkins said as he pronounced the death sentence that he was satisfied she had carried on her wicked trade for a long time. As it was suspected that she might attempt to kill herself while awaiting execution if given the chance, she was kept under close observation, with two female warders watching her by day, and three by night. Even so, she tried to commit suicide at least once while apparently asleep, by attempting to strangle herself under the blanket. Two female warders prevented her just in time.

To Polly, she wrote, 'I have no soul; my soul was hammered out of me in Gloucester Asylum.' This was widely quoted in the press, and anxious to defend the institution, the medical superintendent involved, Mr F. Hurst Craddock, forwarded a letter written to him by Mrs Dyer on 23 January 1895, saying she would never forget the kindness he and his staff had shown her while she was there.

On 5 June she received a final visit from Polly, although there is no record as to what conversation passed between them. The next day the governor of Newgate Gaol was served with a subpoena ordering Mrs Dyer to appear as a witness at her daughter's forthcoming trial. This made little sense, as her execution was due to take place a week before the trial. Moreover, in law it was deemed that a prisoner under sentence of death was legally dead, and therefore any evidence she might give at her the trial would be inadmissible. On 9 June, she was told that all charges against her daughter had been dropped. Mrs Palmer was still ordered to appear before the Berkshire Assizes, but as the Treasury offered no evidence against her, the case was dismissed.

Mrs Dyer was hanged by James Billington at Newgate Prison on 10 June. She had told the prison staff that she would never walk to the scaffold. When the time came, she seemed in a dazed condition, and had to be supported by female officers the few yards from the cell to the drop.

In the afternoon a sale was held of the contents of her last home, 45 Kensington Road, Reading. A collection of items, including a quilt on which she was working at the time of her arrest, a child's cradle in which many of her victims had doubtless slept, and an armchair made by Palmer, raised the sum of £7 15s 3d.

A rhyme was later widely circulated around Reading:

> The old baby farmer, the wretched Miss Dyer
> At the Old Bailey her wages is paid.
> In times long ago, we'd 'a' made a big fy-er
> And roasted so nicely that wicked old jade.

Her conviction led to several changes in the law, including stricter adoption laws designed to reduce and eventually eliminate baby farming altogether. A new Infant Life Protection Act the following year gave local authorities the remit to identify and supervise the nursing and adoption of infants under their jurisdiction, with inspectors appointed to visit any residences they suspected might be houses of confinement or baby farms, and remove any children whom they thought were being abused. Personal advertisements in newspapers were also henceforth subject to greater scrutiny.

Nevertheless, on 13 September 1898, two years after Amelia Dyer's execution, railway workers inspecting carriages at Newton Abbot, Devon, heard a child's cry and found a parcel. Inside was a three-week-old girl, cold and wet but still alive. The daughter of a widow, Jane Hill, she had been given to a Mrs Stewart for £12. The latter had picked up the baby at Plymouth, and apparently dumped her on the next train. On 14 September 'Mrs Stewart' and her husband were traced to Brize Norton and arrested. They were Polly and Arthur Palmer.

ENDNOTES

[1] Harold was taken into the Hendon Union Workhouse in May 1896, probably just before the trial. Aged two years, he was already seriously ill. He died on 11 July, the cause of death being given as stomatitis, attributed to severe malnutrition, low levels of hygiene, and general neglect.

[2] After the trial Jane Smith returned to the workhouse at Bristol, where she died in 1901.

18

'YOU MUST GO NOW, YOU *MUST* GO'

Eton, 1912

Eton College has twice witnessed violent death in the last two centuries. The first, in February 1825, resulted from a fight between two boys, which led to a verdict of 'unlawful slaying'. Neither murder nor manslaughter, the case was thrown out of court. The second, eighty-seven years later, was a very different matter.

Annie Wentworth was a domestic servant working for Mr Booker, a master at Cotton Hall House, Eton Wick Road. After her first period of employment there she left in December 1907, at the end of the autumn term, but returned in August 1912.

By then she was courting a man named Eric Sedgwick. They first met in January 1908 while he was a soldier with the Durham Light Infantry, shortly before being posted to India. He returned to England four years later, was discharged (honourably, as far as records show), and found work as a house porter at the National Liberal Club in London. The couple were soon reunited, and by this time he was aged twenty-seven, while she was twenty-four. If they had not become engaged, they were probably very close to taking such a step.

However, Annie quickly saw another side to the dashing young former army officer. He was very possessive, with a fierce temper, and liable to become violent if thwarted. On 5 October he sent her a telegram telling her he was coming to London, and asked her to meet him at some particular place. As she could not leave Eton she was unable to make the appointment. A few hours later, he turned up at Cotton Hall House in a bad mood. He was obviously not used to people disobeying him, even though Annie's reason for not meeting him was perfectly legitimate. After arriving between 5 and 6 p.m., they went out together at about 8.15 and returned two hours later. On their return Annie was very upset, and as soon as she saw her friend Edith Armstrong, the head housemaid at Eton, she burst into tears.

Twelve days later Sedgwick sent Annie's mother a postcard, addressed 'To all at home'. It included the words:

I can assure you on one vital point ... if Annie and myself keep it up like we have done to-night, Sedgwick will never marry ... You will think this is a funny p.c., but I feel like it to-night. I went down whistling, and came back cursing. Why? Because there's something about Annie.

A letter to Annie, thought to have been written at about the same time, left her in no doubt of Eric's affection for her:

I love you madly, and straight or otherwise nothing will alter that pure feeling which makes me risk everything to have you with me, and to have you in my arms, and then to forget everything in the world. That is real, downright, sheer happiness to have your sweet face against mine.

The same letter carried another, slightly more troubled passage:

I don't believe you could change, dearest, and I don't want you to change. I want you. I know you have been true to me, dear heart, and it was only my body which was untrue to you ... I hope things have ceased worrying you. You need not have worried, for you said nothing should separate us, even if you were true to me, for we should be together dead.

On 10 November Eric went to Eton again and took Annie out in the evening, before bringing her back to the house and returning to London. The next morning, she was very subdued and told Miss Armstrong that she had done something that would 'worry me until my grave'. While they had been together she had 'surrendered herself' to Eric. Afterwards he confessed that he had been unfaithful to her, and she was about to write to him saying it was all over between them. She never wanted to see him again as long as she lived.

On 19 November he replied that he still loved her dearly and begged for forgiveness. She would not change her mind, insisting that she would have nothing more to do with him.

Refusing to take no for an answer, he came back to Eton on 24 November, arriving at around 4 p.m. Edith answered the door and went to tell Annie that he had arrived. Annie, Edith said later, 'appeared very frightened, went as white as death, and trembled very much.' She asked Edith to accompany her downstairs, and, after doing so, Edith went into the pantry next to the servants' hall. Sedgwick and Annie were talking loudly, and after ten minutes Edith went into the hall, apparently to fetch something. This was quite probably a ruse just to let them know that she was nearby in case any unpleasant developments were about to take place. They were both standing by the fireplace, and between sobs Annie said clearly to Sedgwick, 'You must go now, you *must* go.' Edith did not hear Sedgwick say anything in reply, and she told Annie gently not to cry.

She then went upstairs for a few minutes, and on coming down again saw Mrs Booker and one of the maids, who beckoned to her to come quickly. On entering the hall again, Edith saw Annie lying on a chair, bleeding from a wound to the left breast, with Sedgwick leaning over her.

'Eric, Eric, what have you done?' she cried. 'You have killed her!'

Eton College, with the statue of King Henry VI in front.

Eton College buildings from the north.

'For God's sake, Edith, fetch some water,' he answered. He was supporting Annie, who was moaning but appeared to be unconscious. 'They shall not part us,' he kept saying, as he repeatedly kissed her.

Edith then went out to the back gate to see if a policeman was within sight, but without success. As she returned to the hall she saw several of the other maids, some of whom were undoing the front of Annie's dress so they could bathe the wound. Unhappily, it was too late, for within fifteen minutes of the attack Annie was dead. By then the police had been called, and as Sedgwick was arrested, he cried out, 'For God's sake, why can't somebody stop the bleeding?' He was taken to Eton police station, still bearing the telltale signs of blood on his right hand.

That same night Edith showed the local police inspector Annie's box, from which he removed several recently written letters as evidence. The next day Dr Wilfred Attlay of Eton carried out a post-mortem, at which he confirmed that the cause of death was a wound to the heart.

Sedgwick went on trial for wilful murder at Aylesbury Assizes on 15 January 1913 under Mr Justice Bankes, with Sir Ryland Adkins, a barrister and Liberal MP for Middleton, and Drysdale Woodcock for the prosecution, and Bernard Campion for the defence. The main witness for the prosecution was Edith Armstrong, who had known Annie Wentworth since 1908 and recounted Sedgwick's recent visits to her at Eton. Two other maids who had been present on the afternoon of the killing, Emily Mills and Elizabeth Saunders, also testified to having heard screaming in the hall, and described the scene after the victim had been stabbed. Dr Attlay said that the depth of the wound was about two to three inches, and to inflict such a wound would require a certain amount of force.

Mr Campion did not call any witnesses for the defence. Addressing the jury, he argued that there were many degrees of insanity, and there were several cases in which men lost their mental balance to the extent of suddenly giving way to the committal of an act about which they had no knowledge a short while afterwards. He asked them to believe that when Annie Wentworth met her death, Sedgwick was incapable of realising what he was doing. Although it was undeniable that he had committed the crime, as he was alone with the girl at the time, he (Campion) wanted to draw attention to the evident affection between prisoner and deceased. That Sedgwick had a return-half railway ticket, a parcel of chocolate, and some violets in his pocket, showed that there was no deliberate intention to murder the young lady. Moreover, his conduct, particularly bending over her, kissing her and speaking to her, showed how emotional he was – a characteristic of those afflicted with temporary insanity.

In summing up, the judge disagreed with the counsel for the defence in maintaining that prisoner and deceased were always on affectionate terms. Many of the letters seemed to suggest otherwise. The fact that Sedgwick was carrying a knife with him also suggested some degree of premeditation.

The jury were only out for ten minutes before delivering a verdict of guilty. When asked if he had anything to say why sentence of death should not be passed on him, Sedgwick said:

> There have been a great many points advanced as to why this thing was committed. I applied for counsel to defend me and to help me in what has been a very hard thing for me. I gave points to counsel to settle the questions regarding the quarrels that were supposed to have taken place between my sweetheart and myself. I deny before this sentence is passed on me, and I shall before punishment is inflicted on me, that such a thing as a quarrel ever took place between her and me. I know it is no excuse, and I make this statement simply to clear her name and myself. There was never any intention on my part to kill my sweetheart. I am responsible for her death; the law demands satisfaction, and when that law carries out its sentences, I shall go to her with the full knowledge that when she died I did not wilfully kill her. I ask you to accept the statement that there was no quarrel between us, no jealousy or lust.

The judge told Sedgwick that the jury's verdict of wilful murder was, he thought, the only one at which they could arrive, 'having regard to their oath'. The sentence of death he was going to pass 'is not mine; it is the sentence ordained by law'. As Sedgwick left the dock, he was heard crying, 'And may the Lord have mercy on those who brought me to this.'

While in Reading Gaol awaiting execution he reached his twenty-eighth birthday. During his last days, he wrote a letter to the governor, who read part of it out at the conclusion of the inquest. One paragraph he thought was particularly relevant:

Before I take leave of you in this world I wish to state that the statement I made at my trial was the truth. Circumstances of which no explanation has been given brought about a momentary lapse, in which I caused the death of that person most dear to me. Passionately fond of my sweetheart, with her died all my hopes in this world, and I have not a desire to live. My death satisfies the laws of this country, and, willingly given, may be some atonement in the sight of God. I desire to thank you and all other officials who have had me in their charge for the kindness extended to me during my stay in the prison.

Fully resigned to his fate, Sedgwick was hanged on 4 February 1913 at Reading Gaol by John Ellis.

19

'THEY ARE THE CAUSE OF THIS'

Gallows Tree Common, near Pangbourne, 1922

Sarah Blake was landlady of the Crown and Anchor at the hamlet of Gallows Tree Common. Aged fifty-five, she lost her husband towards the end of 1921 but continued to run the hostelry on her own. She was a popular figure, much liked and respected by customers for miles around, and known as one who would take no nonsense from the occasional troublesome character who might come through her doors.

Early in the evening of 2 March 1922 Sarah had a chat with Mrs Payne, her neighbour, who had come into the bar to see her. Mrs Blake was planning to go away the following morning on business for a while, and Mrs Payne had undertaken to look after the inn in her absence. Mrs Payne noticed that the place was empty except for fifteen-year-old Jack Hewett, a farm hand, who was enjoying a soft drink at one of the tables.

Shortly before 8 o'clock that evening Harry Dowling, a farm labourer, went with his father and brother to the inn for a drink. When they arrived, they found the premises closed and in total darkness so they went to the Reformation, another hostelry only a short walk away. Jack Hewett had returned home and been sent by his stepfather Albert back to the Crown and Anchor for some beer. Jack was away for a long time, and on returning said the inn was closed, so he had to walk to the Reformation instead. Later on a young couple also tried Sarah Blake's premises and likewise came away disappointed.

The next morning, at about 8.30, Mrs Payne went back to see her friend. Pushing open the unlocked door, the first thing she saw, to her horror, was Sarah Blake's body lying on the parlour floor, with blood covering the doors, cupboards and ceiling. She had been beaten and stabbed, and her throat had been cut. Mrs Payne fetched her husband, Alfred, at once, and they called the police. Constable Buswell of Rotherfield Peppard arrived, followed shortly after by Dr Gandy, who confirmed that the throat injury had been the cause of death. Sarah had been stabbed several times in what must have been a frenzied attack, her killer using a knife with a broken point, and it had taken place between 6 p.m. and 8 p.m. the previous evening.

Several police officers came to Gallows Tree Common to hunt for the murder weapon or weapons. Constable Russell found the front door key, and Constable Grant saw a bucket of discoloured water in the yard of the inn, which was unfortunately poured away afterwards. The officer described it as a light brown colour consistent with blood, though it was later suggested that it might equally be consistent with discolouration caused by ale glasses being washed in it.

After a few days of enquiries which seemed to lead nowhere, officers from Scotland Yard were brought in. Superintendent Wastie, Inspector Heldon and Sergeant Ryan set up headquarters at Caversham police station.

On 9 March, Constable Hudson noticed Jack Hewett staring into the hedge beside the inn. At first he thought nothing of it, but it occurred to him that this was the same hedge which had been combed by several officers on two previous occasions.

Within hours the police had their first breakthrough. Wastie was called from the scene of the crime by an officer with a message to come to Caversham immediately as a man had confessed to the murder.

The man was Frederick Alfred Sheppard, a labourer and convicted burglar. He lived at 65 Rupert Street, Reading, and had been arrested earlier in the week for a break-in at Victoria Square, nearby. Approaching the constable on duty on the second night of his imprisonment, he had admitted to being one of two men involved in the murder of Sarah Blake. Now he wanted an arrangement which would involve the police dropping the Victoria Square case in return for information on the Crown and Anchor murder.

The Reformation, Gallows Tree Common. (© Colin Bates)

Right: *Sarah Blake.*

Far right: *Frederick Sheppard.*

When interviewed by police, Sheppard said he had been drinking late in Henley on 3 March, and as he had very little money on him he decided he would walk back to Reading, a distance of about eight miles. On his way he met a man named Jack Larkins, who, like him, was always on the lookout for any ready money, whether legal or not. When they reached the Crown and Anchor, Larkins suggested they ought to break in. Sheppard did not favour the idea, but as Larkins was adamant, with some reluctance he accepted the role of look-out. Larkins made his way in through an upstairs window. Shortly afterwards came a scream, the sound of a struggle, then that of somebody being struck repeatedly. Minutes later Larkins reappeared, covered in blood, and a thoroughly frightened Sheppard decided to have nothing more to do with his new acquaintance.

When Superintendent Wastie asked Sheppard what time the two men arrived at the inn, Sheppard said it was about 4 a.m. Wastie told him he was lying, and was not to waste his time any further. The time discrepancy, and the lack of any signs of a burglary, ruled him out. Sheppard was remanded in custody until 4 April, but the elusive and possibly fictitious Larkins was never traced, and charges against Sheppard were not dropped until 5 May.

In mid-March Constable Rippington discovered a knife under the hedgerow near the Crown and Anchor. Hidden under leaves, it had a broken point, and was covered in blood with some hairs attached. This reminded Constable Hudson of having seen Hewett staring at the hedge, and he informed Inspector Heldon. The knife was passed on to Home Office analyst, John Webster. Sergeant Ryan was then sent to Hewett's house and returned with a brown-stained tunic, which was also forwarded to Webster along with a door knocker, some blood-soaked sheets of paper, and Mrs Blake's woolen shawl. Webster returned every item, stating that he could identify Mrs Blake's blood on all the other samples, but was unsure of the stains on the tunic. They were certainly bloodstains, though he was unsure if they were those of Mrs Blake, or indeed how old they were.

Next, Buswell took the knife to Jack Hewett to ask him if he knew anything about it. He denied all knowledge of it, and his stepfather said he had never seen it among the boy's possessions. Buswell then went to see one of Hewett's friends, Joseph Haynes, a farm foreman, who said Hewett owned the knife; he had often seen him using it, and Hewett had sometimes lent it to him.

On 4 April, Superintendent Wastie, accompanied by Inspector Heldon and Sergeant Ryan, went to Padwick Farm, where Hewett worked for 12s per week. He was questioned for two hours by the three detectives, and denied that he had been staring over the hedge at the spot where the knife was found, as well as denying ownership of the knife. The blood on his tunic, he said, was not that of Mrs Blake, but from chickens and rabbits, which he often killed as part of his work on the farm. Nevertheless, he was arrested and taken to Caversham police station, where he was charged with Sarah Blake's murder – and confessed.

Under further questioning by Constable Buswell, who took down a statement, the boy said he had called to see Mrs Blake. She allowed him to pour himself a glass of raspberry champagne and then a glass of ginger stout. At 6 p.m. Alf Payne came in and then left, shortly after which his wife came in for a few minutes. When Hewett and Mrs Blake were alone, Hewett told police that:

> I picked up a piece of iron and hit her with it, and there was a struggle. The lamp was knocked over and the glass broken. I do not remember what happened after that. There was blood on my hands. I went out of the house, locked the street door, and went towards home. I threw my knife, which had bloodstains on it, into the hedge, and threw the keys into the garden. I do not know where I threw the piece of iron. I am very sorry it happened, and do not know what made me do it.

He also said that he took out his knife and stabbed his victim repeatedly, slit her throat to make sure she was dead, and washed his hands in a bucket of water in the yard (this was the bucket that had casually been emptied by a police officer, thus carelessly destroying potentially important evidence), he then went back inside and took 2d from the till, which had contained about £3 in total. His motive was, therefore, obviously not robbery. On his way home he spent the money on dates at a grocery in Gallows Tree Common. The grocer, Mr J. Smith, was contacted and confirmed that the boy had purchased the dates there.

Hewett then signed the confession with apparent relief. When asked why he had done it, he said he wished he had never been to the pictures; 'they are the cause of this,' and he did not know what had made him strike Mrs Blake, but when he did so he could not help himself. He often went to the cinema, and this was thought to have been the one of the first instances where a movie-goer had been so influenced by what he saw on the screen that he went out and committed an act of violence.

Released on bail, Hewett was ordered to appear at Caversham Police Court on 5 May. Arthur Septon Cohen conducted the case for the prosecution, and Mr Gush appeared for the defence. It was only a formality, prior to the main trial at Oxford Assizes. Some evidence was given by police and medical experts. A witness for the prosecution was Eliza Wheeler, of 29 Gallows Tree Common, near the Crown and Anchor. She recalled that about two days before the murder she had been in the bar parlour when she heard Mrs Blake say such things as, 'Take more care in future, young man,' and 'Please remember next time, Jack.' Mr Gush asked why, if there had been a row between Mrs Blake and Hewett only two days previously, was he in the Crown and Anchor drinking – and a drink which she had given him. It hardly seemed like the behaviour of two people who were not getting on with each other. He then asked Miss Wheeler if it was not true that there had been differences between the Wheelers and the Hewetts for some time, but she denied this.

The magistrates then decided to adjourn the case to Oxford Assizes, but not before Mr Gush told the court he was concerned with the way in which Scotland Yard had treated his client. The young man, he went on, had made a statement of confession which he had since withdrawn. Was it moral, he asked, or even ethical, for three experienced police officers, Heldon, Wastie and Ryan, to question a boy of fifteen for several long hours without him having any legal representation, and then to take him to Caversham police station where further enquiries were made by Constable Buswell? It was no wonder that a frightened boy would confess to almost anything under such circumstances. With this, the proceedings came to an end.

The case was heard at Oxford Assizes on 2 June before Mr Justice Shearman, with J.B. Matthews KC and Graham Millward for the prosecution, and Mr E.C. Gates for the defence. Harry Dowling and his brother described how the inn had been closed when they went to visit, after which Alf Payne and his wife gave evidence of Hewitt's presence in the bar at 6.15, as well as of the discovery of Sarah Blake's body the next morning. Medical evidence was forwarded by Dr Bernard Spilsbury and others. Constables Grant, Russell, Hudson and Rippington gave practical evidence concerning the pail of water and the knife, and the latter was also identified by Joseph Haynes. The last of the civilian witnesses was Mr Smith, who had sold Hewett the dates.

Next came testimony from Inspector Heldon, Superintendent Wastie, Sergeant Ryan and Constable Buswell regarding the confession. Mr Gates said unequivocally that the police had obtained it in peculiar circumstances to say the least, inferring that Hewett had been interrogated rather than questioned, and had been as good as bullied into signing a statement by Constable Buswell at Caversham.

On behalf of the Home Office, Dr Spilsbury said there were over sixty wounds and bruises on the head and shoulders of the deceased. There were four fractures of the skull, and a deep cut to the neck, which, rather than being the result of a single stab, must have been caused by working the knife around in the wound. When

Jack Hewitt.

cross-examined, he said he would not consider these wounds were necessarily the work of a man and not of a boy. He thought a strong boy would be easily capable of inflicting them.

When Hewett took the stand, he denied having done any harm to Mrs Blake. He had left her at 6.20 p.m. in the best of health, returned at 8 p.m. to find the inn in darkness, and he knew nothing else. When questioned by Mr Matthews, he said he had never owned or even seen the knife before, and that he had made the statement at Caversham because he was terrified. To Mr Gates, he said he had been in the lavatory much of the time when Buswell wrote out the statement. When the officer gave it to him to read and sign, there were many words he did not understand or could not read.

The final questions put by the prosecution concerned whether it was possible that anybody else, other than the defendant, might have committed this crime. Matthews thought it very unlikely, and went on to make much of the knife and the confession. In his final address, Gates said eloquently that if one ignored the rightly controversial confession, one was left with almost nothing in the case. The metal bar had not been found, and they only had the knife, which both the defendant and his father asserted that he never owned. They only had the word of Joseph Haynes for it, and this was surely insufficient evidence on which to base a conviction for a crime as serious as murder. Finally he described the state of mind of Hewett that day. He had returned home behaving quite normally, and surely a boy of fifteen could not have committed murder and then returned home showing no signs of stress?

After a lengthy summing-up by Mr Justice Shearman, the jury retired at 2 p.m. and returned thirty minutes later with a unanimous verdict of guilty. The judge said that the law prevented him from announcing the death penalty for one so young, and instead sentenced Jack Hewitt to be detained at His Majesty's pleasure.

20

'WE CANNOT FACE LIFE ANY LONGER'

Maidenhead, 1929

Heywood Park, a hamlet in White Waltham, near Maidenhead, was the scene of several grim deaths, some deliberate and some accidental, in the first half of the twentieth century. To many these were no more than mere coincidence, but others saw them as the legacy of a curse which had its origin in events several centuries earlier. White Waltham was named after Waltham Abbey in Essex. In 1275 the Abbot of Waltham was Reginald de Maidenheth, a Berkshire man. He took a dislike to a woman whom he accused of witchcraft, had her arrested, and ordered that a gallows should be erected in Cannon Lane where she could be hanged without trial. Her body was cut down after death and buried there.

Soon after the coming of the railway age, deaths began to occur with such frequency that the superstitious attributed them to the witch's curse. In 1905 a passenger boarded at Paddington for the westcountry. At White Waltham he got out of his seat for no apparent reason, opened the door of the carriage train while it was still travelling at high speed, and fell on to the rails. His body, minus a leg, and the contents of his suitcase were later retrieved from alongside the track. Eight years later, at more or less the same spot, a maintenance crew found a headless body, so badly mutilated that identification proved impossible. In 1929 the body of Hilda Craig was found on the line, minus her head and arms. The following year a platelayer was killed after stepping in front of an oncoming train, and in 1935 the headless body of William Cullinford of Swindon was found on the track. At his inquest a witness said that he was subject to fainting fits, but a verdict of suicide was returned.

To this unhappy catalogue must be added two murders during the same period, those of Mrs Goldup and Mrs Warren (*see* page 134-42).

In April 1929 Percy and Jessie Goldup moved into Elms End, a bungalow at Heywood Park. Percy was aged thirty-six, his wife forty-eight. He had been a baker, although whether he was working at the time is not clear, and had a history of severe depression. Between August 1928 and February 1929 the couple had taken lodgings with Maria Hipsey at her house in Norfolk Road, Reading. She found Percy's increasingly eccentric behaviour was making him a liability, and after he accused Mrs Hipsey of trying to chloroform him, she asked the couple to leave.

The Goldups were known as early risers, and on Saturday 26 April their milkman, Alexander Kirby, knocked on their door at 8.15 a.m. to collect the weekly money. There was no reply, which he found puzzling. In fact they had got up earlier that day, as they were seen by Aubrey Irving of Fern Cottage, Furze Platt, who was tending the garden of a nearby cottage. At 7.30 a.m., he had seen Mrs Goldup come out of the house to collect some washing, and watched her husband follow her as he went to the shed.

During his lunch break, soon after 1 p.m., Kirby went back to the bungalow, but could not hear any movement or see any signs of life. Keen to secure his payment, he went back two hours later, and a fourth time at 6.30 p.m. By this time he suspected all was not well, and he decided to try and look through the curtains for any telltale signs of life. To his horror, on peering a little way into the bedroom and the hallway, he noticed blood everywhere.

He went at once to alert the police, his nearest contact being Constable Frank Fraser of White Waltham. Both men returned to the bungalow together, and Fraser was punctilious in following procedure. He knocked on the door and called briefly before forcing an entrance through the bedroom window. Once inside, they were confronted by the sight of a bedroom and hall deluged in blood, with the bodies of a man and woman lying in their nightclothes on the neatly made bed, their throats cut. The man was still breathing, but the woman, who also had substantial head wounds and had bled far more profusely, was obviously dead.

Fraser sent for an ambulance, a local doctor, and his superior officer, Inspector Henry Brown of Maidenhead. Apart from the bloodstains, the house was unusually tidy, with no sign of a forced entry or struggle. Robbery had obviously not been a motive.

In the hall Fraser found a bloodstained hammer, and at the bedside was a cut-throat razor with part of the blade missing.

Woodlands Park Road, White Waltham, Maidenhead. (© Andrew Smith).

AIDENHEAD BUNGALOW TRAGEDY.—The Heywood's Park bungalow, "Elms En here a terrible discovery was made last week-end. Mrs. Jessie Goldup was found d and her husband had extensive wounds in the throat. Their photographs are inset

Elms End, Heywood Park, Maidenhead, the scene of Jessie Goldup's death at the hands of her husband, Percy.

There was also a note addressed to Mr Goldup's mother. When Brown arrived, Fraser handed it to him. It read:

> We have desired to die together. We cannot face life any longer. I hope God will spare you to live to a great age.

This shortened version was later published in the papers. An additional portion, suppressed for obvious reasons, stated that he had come to his end through nobody else but Jessie, and Edie and her husband 'was at the bottom of all this.'

Dr Doherty found that Jessie had sustained a fractured skull, and the weapon involved was the hammer in the hall, but the wound which had killed her was the razor slash across the windpipe. When the doctor examined Percy, she found a five-inch gash across the throat with the missing part of the razor still embedded in the wound. He was rushed to hospital, and as soon as he was in a fit state, he was interviewed by Inspector Brown.

On 28 May he was charged under his full name of Percy Robert James Goldup with the murder of his wife, Jessie Statham Goldup, at Maidenhead Magistrates'

Court. Doctors were brought in to testify to his state of mind. As the Reading Assizes were too busy, and it was thought as well to have the trial somewhere where there would be a speedy resolution, the trial was fixed for Oxford Assizes on 7 June. It was presided over by Mr Justice Shearman, with Mr A.J. Long for the prosecution, and Mr A.F. Clements for the defence. Goldup pleaded not guilty to murder, and spent much of the trial in tears.

Following preliminary evidence, the court looked at the Goldups' past. Edith Jane Snow, wife of Charles Snow and sister of Jessie Goldup, who lived in Hill Street, Reading, was brought as a witness. On being examined by Mr Long, she informed the court that her sister had married Goldup sixteen years previously, and despite the age gap between husband and wife, she was sure they had been happily married and went everywhere together. They had previously lived in Reading and she confirmed that they only took up residence in Maidenhead a fortnight earlier.

Then Mr Long, noticing that her husband's middle name was Jesse, asked if her husband was ever known thus. She replied that he was always known as Charles. He then asked if her sister was known as Jesse, to which she replied that she always was. Mr Long then asked Mrs Snow if she and her husband had lent the prisoner and his wife some money. She replied that they had indeed lent the Goldups some, and they were keen to be repaid. Nevertheless, the situation had not caused any ill-feeling between them.

When cross-examined by Mr Clements for the defence, Edith Snow stated that Goldup had lost £50 which he had invested in the bungalow. For a long time he had suffered from depression, and she was sure that he was mentally ill as he had been heard to say that he believed he had vapours and fumes around him, and that they were choking him. In answer to another question from Mr Clements, the witness stated that when she and Charles had visited the bungalow at White Waltham, Percy had taken her into the garden and given her a graphic description of the choking vapours. He also told her that the police were watching him and that everybody was against him. He also said he thought he would not be alive for much longer.

Since the time of the offence, Percy had been held in custody at Brixton Prison. The next witness was Dr Watson, senior medical officer at the prison. He said that in his opinion the prisoner was suffering from manic depression and insane melancholia. He had had long conversations with Goldup and was sure that his claim of amnesia since the event was genuine, as when things became too difficult for such people, the mind was inclined to blot them out completely. During long conversations with the prisoner, there had been no mention of any quarrel or jealousy between husband and wife. The doctor believed that as far as he was aware it had been a happy marriage, and Goldup seemed to be a devoted husband.

He was followed in the witness box by Mrs Hipsey, who spoke of her experiences with the couple at Reading. Next was Dr Michael Murphy of London Street, Reading.

He informed the court that he was Goldup's local doctor, had worked for some years in a mental asylum, and was sure the prisoner was badly depressed and mentally ill. In answer to a question from Mr Clements, he told the court that he was quite sure Goldup was in a condition where he could murder his wife and remember nothing about it a short time afterwards.

Mr Justice Shearman then asked Dr Murphy to stand down. He then called learned counsel together; spoke to them briefly, dismissed them and turned to the jury, directing them to bring in a verdict of 'guilty but insane'. Once this was done, he sentenced Percy Goldup to be detained at His Majesty's pleasure. The prisoner left the court weeping, a broken man, to spend the rest of his days as an inmate in Broadmoor.

21

DEATH OF A
TOBACCONIST

Reading, 1929

On 22 June 1929, at about 6.15 p.m., sixty-year-old Alfred Oliver was behind the counter as usual in his tobacconist's shop at 15 Cross Street, Reading, situated in a narrow thoroughfare between Broad Street and Station Road. At that time of day the street was generally fairly quiet, though most of the other shops were open, including various grocers' and butchers' establishments. His wife, Annie, had just gone out to do some shopping of her own. Husband and wife, who had been married for about nine years, were looking forward to a holiday in Penzance the following week. The holiday never took place.

A customer came into the shop to buy some cigarettes or tobacco, and tendered a half-crown. Mr Oliver turned round to take a packet from the shelf, and bent down over the till for change. The customer attacked him with a heavy instrument, helped himself to the contents of the till, £12 10*s*, and left. Mrs Oliver returned a few minutes later to find her husband slumped semi-conscious behind the counter, blood pouring from his head, which was bent down over his chest. She spoke to him, but he was unable to answer. The police were called, and Constable Mogford sent a message to Scotland Yard with details of the attack. He also informed the Yard that at 6 p.m. two fur coats and a small brown attaché case containing ladies' clothes and toilette set had been stolen from a car in Broad Street. The suspect was a man aged between thirty and forty, wearing a blue suit, clean-shaven with a red face, and with a Scottish accent. They had reason to believe that the same man was responsible for the theft and the assault on Alfred Oliver.

Mr Oliver was taken to the Royal Berkshire Hospital. When brought in he had regained consciousness, and made a brief statement:

*Broad Street,
Reading, c. 1930.*

*Wokingham Road,
Reading.*

I was in the room behind the counter. Mrs Oliver had gone out, leaving me to clear away the tea. I had an attaché case on the table containing about £30 in notes and silver which I last saw just before tea, when I got some change for a man. I think he was from the gas office.

Later he added that he was in the shop at about 6 o'clock, reading a book, *A Day from London to Penzance*, but could recall no more than that. At around midday on 23 June, Chief Constable Burrows informed Scotland Yard that Mr Oliver was in a critical state, not expected to survive, and they required an officer to help with crime investigation as soon as possible. Two detectives, Jim Berrett and John Harris, came from London to

Reading central police station in Valpy Street to assist. Soon after their arrival, Annie Oliver returned from hospital. After an operation her husband had rallied briefly in the morning, but his mind was still a complete blank, and he had no recollections of the attack. The hospital staff had given up hope, and he died that night. Now the investigation was a murder enquiry.

An inspection of the scene at the shop revealed blood behind the counter, but none on the counter itself or on the floor, as well as broken tobacco scales, Mr Oliver's shattered glasses and broken false teeth. Harris found a bloodstained thumbprint on the showcase, and a spattering of blood where the tobacco, cigarettes and cigars were displayed. Sergeant Pope also found out that around the time of the attack, a passer-by had barged a Mrs Jackson outside the shop. She was traced, but declined to make a statement. As she could not be regarded as a suspect, the police put no pressure on her to do so.

On Monday 24 June, the police went to the Royal Berkshire Hospital to take Oliver's fingerprints for the purpose of identification. A message from Pangbourne police station sent them to go and see a man who claimed to be the murderer, but he was a drunk who clearly had no connection with either offence. When they returned to Reading, they found Sergeant Knight had arrested a thirty-six-year-old man and charged him with the theft of the coats and other property from the car, but after questioning he was eliminated as a murder suspect.

The next day the inquest was held under the coroner, John Lancelot Martin. Opening the proceedings, he spoke of 'a brutal attack on one of our citizens in the heart of our town on a busy Saturday afternoon.' He added that Mr Oliver had been his friend for nearly thirty years, and they had known each others' families well. 'I helped him to tide over his troubles and he helped me tide over mine; so you can imagine my feelings.'

It was revealed that before he had died at 5.50 p.m. on 23 June, Mr Oliver told the police that he could remember nothing about the attack. Nobody was yet certain as to the identity of the weapon. A post-mortem showed thirteen lacerations on the scalp, some on the front of the head and others on the back of the skull, and six lacerations around the left ear. He had a cut on the left jaw and one on the right side of the face near the lips, and his right eye was severely bruised. There was also severe bruising on the left side of his neck, and a small bruise on the back of his right hand, as well as three large fractures of the walls of the skull, and three complete fractures at the base of the skull, and lower and upper jaw on the right side. The cause of death was multiple fractures of the skull associated with severe contusion to the brain.

Dr Joyce said a heavy instrument, possibly two, must have been used to strike the victim. A heavy implement would have been required to fracture the base of the skull, and the small wound could hardly have been produced by a blunt one. It might have been an instrument with two edges, with a heavy side and a sharp side. A rain of blows had probably been inflicted, each wound representing a blow. 'Would a tyre lever do it?' asked the coroner. The doctor said he thought it would, and it might produce some of the wounds, but he did not think it would result in that kind of fracture of the skull. A large hammer may have been used. He was not clear about the six lacerated wounds round the left ear, as they might have been produced by a heavy hammer or something flat, such as a spanner.

The coroner then adjourned proceedings. He wanted to leave the matter in the capable hands of Chief Inspector Berrett, his assistant and the local police, and reconvene the court when there was enough evidence for the coroner to be able to deliver a verdict. Before dismissing everyone, he made an appeal on behalf of the police authorities to the press, asking for anyone who could supply information to assist the police, including those who may have a mysterious person or persons staying with them or who have calling at their shop, or noticed anybody suspicious in Cross Street, or anyone with blood on his hands shortly after 6.30 p.m. on 22 June, to contact either the Reading chief constable, New Scotland Yard, or their nearest police station, as soon as possible. If any shopkeeper had sold an implement which might have been used in the attack, would he likewise contact the police.

Later that day, Scotland Yard issued a message stating that at about 1.45 p.m. on 22 June a Mr Percy Taylor had handed Mr Oliver a cheque in the shop, drawn from Barclays Bank at the local branch in Station Road. It had not been presented, and was missing from the shop premises. An appeal was issued, quoting the number and value (£1) and asking anybody through whose hands it had passed, or was found uttering or presenting it, to contact the police, but nobody came forward.

Three days after the murder, twenty-one-year-old George Jefferies, who lived ten minutes' walk away, in Castle Street, reported that he was in the shop at around the time of the attack. He told Berrett he had left his work as a messenger early to visit his sister, who was very ill in hospital. After taking parcels to the post office at 6 p.m., he called in at the shop for cigarettes at 6.08 with a half-crown in his hand. As nobody answered him when he entered the shop, he looked over the counter and saw the legs of a man. Leaning further over the counter, he saw as far as the man's waist, and noticed some blood alongside. It was Mr Oliver, twitching and moaning. He was

so startled that he left at once, stood on the pavement for a few minutes wondering what to do, but as there was nobody else around the time, he went straight home.

Royal Berkshire Hospital, London Road, Reading. (© Andrew Smith)

Two of his friends, Mr Hart and Mr Hendley, were also quizzed at the police station that evening in separate rooms, and a discrepancy in the story emerged. Jefferies said he did not have his messenger's bicycle with him during the incident, but he told his friends he had run out of the shop, leapt on his bike, and made off as fast as he could. Jefferies was allowed to leave the station at 11.30 that evening, having been told his sister was dying, but he would certainly be called back.

Seven days after the attack, Mr Foster, the landlord of the Bull in Cross Street, described an encounter with a man about 5ft 9in. tall, aged between thirty and forty, unshaven, ruddy in complexion, with a broad Scottish accent and wearing a blue suit. He told Scotland Yard detectives that the man knocked on the inn door at about 5.55 p.m., asking to see the secretary of the local Scottish Association, as he needed money urgently. Mr Foster had sent him away empty-handed.

Other witnesses mentioned a man of a similar description. Mrs Shepherd put him at about twenty-five years old, about 5ft 7in. tall, stocky, and wearing a blue suit, seen rushing down Friar Street at about 6.08 p.m., while Mr Rivers saw a dark-suited man running down Cross Street whom he thought to be in his early thirties, and about 6ft tall. At about 6.05 p.m., Mrs Levington was almost knocked over when a tall, fair-haired man shouted at her to 'clear out of the way,' and rushed down Broad Street. Chief Inspector Berrett collected statements from others describing a red-faced man behaving in a peculiar way, and wearing either a blue or a dark suit. Nobody mentioned Jefferies the messenger boy.

More useful was an account given by Alice James, who was walking down Cross Street at about 6.10 p.m. She claimed to have seen a tall man with iron-grey hair standing in the doorway of Mr Oliver's shop, aged about forty, with blood spattered on his face, as if he had just been in a fight or had had a nosebleed. However, she could not recall what he was wearing, and could not pick him out of the Criminal Records Office picture gallery. Meanwhile, Mrs Jackson, previously so reluctant to help, now came forward, told the *Daily News* her story and spoke of a man in a dark blue suit, about 5ft 8in. tall, rushing out of Mr Oliver's shop, colliding with her and shouting, 'I'm sorry,' before rushing off again. More sightings were described, and as well as the suit, the Scottish accent was mentioned more and more.

By 17 July over a hundred witness statements had been given to Berrett. No weapon had yet been found, and no man named. Berrett's description of the suspect was of a middle-aged man with grey hair, fairly respectable appearance, wearing a dark blue suit and no hat, which was unusual in those days.

At around this time Chief Constable Burrows was in the Wellington Club, Friar Street, opposite the Royal County Theatre. One night, a fellow member told him he thought their suspect with grey hair might be the American actor Philip Yale Drew. Aged forty-nine, Drew was starring in a production of *The Monster* at the time of the attack on Oliver. On 19 July Burrows telephoned Berrett and Harris, now back

Cross Street, Reading. (© Andrew Smith)

at Scotland Yard, to say that he thought this might be the breakthrough they had been seeking. By now Drew was playing the part of a detective in a production at the Theatre Royal, Nottingham. A letter was sent to the chief constable of Nottingham to arrange a visit from the Reading and Scotland Yard detectives as soon as possible.

Harris decided to take Jefferies in again and obtain his fingerprints. Mrs Jackson said he was not the man who had bumped into her, but a Mrs Luckett had said that Jefferies had once hit his sister over the head with a jemmy. Harris doubted this statement, but invited Jefferies to talk it over. As he had hoped, Jefferies sat down in the interview room and placed his hands on the table, which had just been covered with clean white paper. Not only did the jemmy incident prove to be hearsay, but also the paper was treated afterwards with a special black powder so that the fingerprints could be matched with a bloodstained print on the shop display case. The prints belonged to a different man.

The senior police officers involved gathered at Nottingham's Guildhall police station, and decided not to disrupt the evening performance at the Theatre Royal to speak to Drew. Instead Sergeant John Harris, representing Superintendent Doubleday of Reading and Sergeant Ellington of Nottingham, went to see him at his lodgings at Fox Road, West Bridgeford, at 9.30 on the morning of 23 July.

Drew was astonished when Harris introduced himself and asked if he would accompany him to the police station to help with their enquiries. His first reaction was one of horror, thinking he was being accused of murder. Harris insisted that this was not the case, and merely required his presence at the station. Once there, Drew was asked to read and sign a statement, confirming that he had been told that he answered the description of a man seen at the scene of the murder and standing in a shop doorway, and had been asked to account for his movements on the day in question. He had also been cautioned that whatever he said would be taken down in writing and may be used as evidence. The same policy with white paper was conducted during the three hours he was being questioned. He maintained his innocence and denied he had ever been anywhere near Cross Street in Reading, let alone any tobacconist. As with Jefferies, his thumbprint did not match that on the showcase.

The next day Drew was called back to the police station for further questioning. He was finding the ordeal very stressful, and claimed that the questioning was seriously affecting him and his work as an actor. While he was being questioned, another police officer was following up a lead to a local cleaning firm to recover his clothes which he had left for cleaning. He was successful in obtaining Drew's blue suit jacket from the cleaning firm and it was sent to Scotland Yard for examination – and Drew was allowed to go.

However, his 'ordeal' was far from over. By 7 August the touring production had moved to St Albans, and Drew was struggling to continue his performances while still being summoned for regular interviews with the police, and he was drinking heavily. Again, he had another three hours of questioning, preceded by the customary caution. His jacket had revealed no bloodstains, only signs of recent chemical cleaning, but he had been unable to produce the matching trousers, which he claimed had disappeared on the day of the attack on Mr Oliver. He said he had packed them in his trunk in his Reading dressing room on the day in question, but when he arrived in Maidstone, the next town on the tour, they were missing. Again he was permitted to leave, knowing he would soon be required again.

Two days later, his blue serge trousers mysteriously reappeared in his dressing room at St Albans, draped across his trunk. He reported this to the police, who took them for examination. They revealed nothing, but Berrett was suspicious of the actor and his apparent inability to recall his movements on the day in question. At this stage Drew was still merely helping the police with their enquiries, and had not been apprehended as a suspect, but the constant questioning was taking its toll on him.

The inquest was due to convene again on 2 October, and opened at 11.25 that morning. After the details were given of Mr Oliver's discovery by his wife and details of what had happened to him, George Jefferies was called in for questioning. He was still unable to give any satisfactory reason for his hesitation in coming forward after discovering Mr Oliver wounded in the shop. 'I didn't know what to do,' he admitted. 'I didn't think it was anything serious until I saw it in the papers.' When it made the news, he was frightened to come forward as he feared losing his job. His mother then told the court that when he arrived home afterwards, he sat on the sofa with his head in his hands, telling her he had been 'scared to death'. There were no marks on his clothes which he was wearing on his return. As he was still very upset on the Monday, and unable to touch his food, she suggested he should tell the police everything, and he said he wished he had done so. The reason she herself had not given information was because of the imminent death of a sister.

Next in the witness box was a local butcher, Mr Loxton, whose shop was next door but one to that of Mr Oliver. He said that at 1.30 p.m. on 22 June a man, who might have been Scottish, Irish or American, came into his shop and asked if he had any liver, then left before he could reply. The butcher saw him again between 5.30 and 6 p.m., looking in the wireless shop opposite the tobacconist's. He started to walk away, looking agitated, then went towards Mr Oliver's shop and disappeared from view.

He described a man 5ft 8in. tall, clean-shaven, no hat, and long untidy dark hair, wearing a navy blue suit, brown shoes, collar and tie. When asked by the coroner if anybody present resembled that man, he pointed to Drew. The coroner asked Drew to stand, and Loxton swore on oath that it was the same man.

The inquest was then adjourned until the following day, and Drew was advised to secure the services of a solicitor. The next day, Alice James gave in court her description of the man with iron-grey hair, apparently wiping blood from his face as he stood in the doorway of the Olivers' shop. She had noticed the time on the town hall clock – it was 6.10 p.m. The coroner asked if such a person was present, and she identified Drew without hesitation. The solicitor asked whether she had really seen him with blood on his face, and she swore that she had. He must have been trying to hide or wipe away an injury, and he was definitely wearing a dark blue suit. Several other witnesses placed him in and around Cross Street on the day in question, conflicting with his assertion to the police in July that he had never visited the street in his life. One, Herbert Booth, said he had accompanied Drew to the Welcome Café in Cross Street at 10.30 a.m. that day, and about three hours later Reginald Barber had shaved him. Again, they confirmed to the coroner that they were certain this was the same man.

The following day, 4 October, Alfred Fry, stage manager for *The Monster*, said that he had heard Drew singing as he entered the stage door at about 6 p.m. on the day in question, though he did not see him. He then saw him at about 6.15 p.m. outside his dressing room in his stage clothes. Mrs Goodhall, Drew's landlady at his King's Meadow Road lodgings, said he had rushed out of the house about 6.10 p.m., which meant that Fry could not have heard him singing. Mrs Goodhall's evidence was supported by two neighbours, Mrs Crouch and Mrs Green, who saw him rushing off from the lodgings at about 6 or 6.10. However, Drew had admitted to her that he could leave her sitting room and be on stage in seven minutes flat, especially as he often ran or walked very fast. Further doubt was placed on his landlady's testimony when she admitted that the clocks in her house were not always particularly reliable.

By Monday 7 October, the next day of proceedings, Drew was visibly showing the strain of being treated, though not yet charged, as a murder suspect. His solicitor advised him that he was appointing a barrister, William Arthur Fearnley-Whittingstall, for the rest of the trial. Increased media attention led to well-wishers and fans of Drew lining the route from the Great Western Hotel, where he was staying, to the court. That morning his missing blue trousers story was relayed in court, and it was noticed that new pockets had recently been sewed into them. This might have been done to eliminate bloodstains, and the police wondered if this was the reason his jacket had gone to the Nottingham cleaners.

On 8 October Drew took the stand and was in the witness box for about one hour and twenty minutes, but his answers were vague and rambling. He could not recall clearly where he was on the day in question, although he was good at remembering his lines on stage. In view of the number of witnesses who swore they had seen him in Cross Street that day, his position looked precarious. The frustrated foreman of the inquest jury even asked him if, in view of his inability to give any explanation of his movements on Saturday 22 June before his arrival at the theatre for the evening performance, he suggested that the sworn testimony of the witnesses as to his movements in regard to Cross Street and to the theatre was perjury? Drew answered that there were so many witnesses against him, and so many differing accounts with regard to the time, that he would not like to say they had committed perjury.

It was fortunate for him that one more witness was to be called. Another local butcher, Alfred John Wells, was tracked down by Bernard O'Donnell, a crime reporter for *Empire News*. Wells had also given a statement to the police concerning a man in a blue suit at the crime scene, but had not been called to give evidence as the police had mislaid his statement and he was not on the witness list. O'Donnell was aware of the statement and had befriended Drew, believing him to be innocent. Under cross-examination, Wells proved concise and articulate when giving evidence. He had seen and spoken to a man in a blue suit at the Welcome Café at 7.30 a.m. on the day of the attack, a man who had a habit of wiping his hand across his face in the manner of the person seen by Mrs James in the Olivers' shop doorway. He saw him again that evening in the Cross Street area at about 5.40 p.m., with a raincoat over his shoulder. His original statement was located and taken to the inquest. It showed Wells had gone to the police station on the night of the crime, and given a full description of the man in the blue suit. He recalled the description precisely in court. William Fearnley-Whittingstall addressed Wells and asked if he would recognise the man again. Drew was asked to stand up, and Wells insisted that this was not the same man, adding that his man in a blue suit had a northern accent.

This concluded the day's proceedings, and by then over sixty witnesses had given evidence. On the following day the coroner summed up, and the jury retired. Excitement outside the court was intense, with crowds eager for the verdict. The jury were out for over two hours before returning. The foreman said that after careful deliberation, they unanimously agreed that the evidence was too conflicting for them to establish the guilt of any particular person, and were returning a verdict of wilful murder against some person or persons unknown. Drew was a free man, though he was angry that he never received any compensation for his mutilated blue suit.

On 5 November Philip Dickins, also known as Joseph Barrett, a forty-five-year-old Glaswegian, walked into a police station and gave himself up as the murderer. He was found to be suffering from delusions, and was moved from the Reading Board of Guardians institution to the Ministry of Pensions Mental Hospital at Cosham. The police were satisfied that not only did he did not commit the crime, but also that he had never been to Reading.

Even before the murder, Drew's heavy drinking had made him a liability, and though exonerated from blame, his acting career never recovered from the scandal. He died in London in 1940 of throat cancer. Nobody else was ever apprehended in connection with the case and the murder of Alfred Oliver remains unsolved.

22

THE BODY UNDER THE BEDDING

Maidenhead, 1932

In 1924, Gwendoline Fleet, a single mother, married Thomas Warren. She already had two children, Marjorie, born in 1916 and Ronald (known as Ronnie), born in 1920, by a previous relationship. They settled at Court View, Maidenhead. To help make ends meet they took in a lodger, and in July 1930 Ernest Hutchinson, a forty-two-year-old bakery assistant, moved in. Gwen, as she was popularly known, was an unashamed flirt, and to Thomas's horror, a day or two later his wife told him that she and the children were leaving him, and starting a new life with Ernest.

A forgiving husband who adored his wife, Thomas was prepared to be patient and let what he hoped was a brief infatuation run its course. About two months later Gwen wrote to him, asking him to forgive her, and offering to return so they could start again. She may or may not have told him that at the start of her fling with Hutchinson she had become pregnant by him, and a daughter, Constance, was born in April 1931. Thomas was prepared to accept this, but the fractured marriage was doomed and, in July 1932, she and the children left Thomas for good. Marjorie, now sixteen, had already moved out. A weary but resigned Thomas returned to his native Burnham, while Gwen went back to Hutchinson and they rented a nearby semi-detached house, Davyholme, in Heywood Park.

About a month after they had settled in, Hutchinson, whose job mainly involved making deliveries for the bakery, was made redundant, and his prospects of finding another appeared minimal. Relations between the couple soured rapidly, and he took to drinking heavily. He was an inveterate smoker, and Gwen told him that if he did not cut back on these indulgences and find himself work again, he would not be allowed to share her bed any longer.

On 10 September Ronnie returned home after running an errand in town, and Hutchinson told him that arrangements had been made for him to go and stay with his aunt, Miss Mabel Fleet, in Burnham. Spinster Mabel, headmistress of East Burnham School, was devoted to her rather flighty sister, although she had long been anxious about her behaviour and the effect it was having on her children.

Hutchinson handed the boy his rail fare, and sent him on his way. Ronnie thought it would just be an overnight stay, and came home a day later. On his return Hutchinson met him at the garden gate, with Constance in his arms. He handed the child to Ronnie, saying their mother had gone to Birmingham to see friends, and he would have to take Connie to Burnham. Collecting his coat, he then escorted them part of the way to the station. Miss Fleet was rather startled to find her nephew and niece on the doorstep again, and thought it unlike her sister to act in this way, as she was devoted to her children and they were virtually inseparable. When Ronnie mentioned the visit to Birmingham, Mabel began to suspect something was not quite right.

At about midday on Sunday 11 September, Joseph Hutton, a former policeman who lived next door to Davyholme, saw Hutchinson in the garden and asked how Gwen was. As she was usually an early riser and it seemed unlike her not to be up yet. Hutchinson said she was still in bed, and 'making a day of it'. Hutton had got to know Gwen quite well and she had confided to him that she was frightened of Hutchinson, sometimes to the extent that she was scared to go to sleep at night. Initially he thought she was exaggerating, but in view of the question marks hanging over her disappearance, he was now not so sure.

On 14 September Miss Fleet received a postcard from Gwen, saying she planned to stay away until Friday, and would she keep the children until then. This went some way towards easing her worries, but even so she decided she would look after Connie and send Ronnie to find out more from Hutchinson. He took a bus back, arrived home about midday and met Hutchinson leaving the house, carrying an attaché case. He told Ronnie he was going to Birmingham to meet his mother, and they would return together on Friday 16 September. Meanwhile Ronnie should return to his aunt's house. He handed the boy a note for Miss Fleet, reading: 'Just a few lines to you saying I am going to Birmingham to Gwen for a few days so no use writing to her until Friday. Keep Ronnie and Connie until then.'

That same day, 12 September, Albert Davis, a dealer in second-hand goods from Bridge Street, Maidenhead, paid Hutchinson £3 16s for a piano, sofa and kitchen table, all of which were delivered to him by hand cart.

Miss Fleet was now so alarmed that she decided to take the children with her and visit Heywood Park herself. They arrived back at about 6.30 p.m. to find the house closed, the doors locked and bolted. Miss Fleet did not want to worry her young nephew, but she was beginning to fear the worst, and knew they would have to break in. They found a larder window had been left slightly open, enabling Ronnie to climb through, go to the back door and let his aunt in. They looked around the house and noticed that the piano, sofa and table had gone. In Ronnie's bedroom the bed was missing, and clothes were strewn untidily around the floor. The room which Gwen had sometimes shared with Ernest was also in a mess, and the bed was unmade.

Remembering that a former police officer lived next door, Miss Fleet decided to speak to him. Hutton confirmed that he had not seen Gwen for three or four days, and agreed to come and look round the house. Once he had gone upstairs and checked the spare bedroom which, thankfully, Miss Fleet had not thought to check herself, it did not take him long to make the dreaded discovery. Bedding was piled up in the corner on top of a single bedstead, with rolled-up bedclothes on top. Underneath was a spring mattress balanced on the metal structure of the top half of a single bed, and a quilt.

As he looked and felt through the heap, preparing himself for the worst, he found Gwen's stone-cold body, barefoot but otherwise fully clothed. Once he had recovered from the shock, he covered her carefully with the quilt, then quickly went downstairs and sent Miss Fleet and Ronnie out of the house in order to spare them from the terrible sight. He then called the Maidenhead police, who brought their own doctor, Dr Wilson.

On 13 September a post-mortem was held at Maidenhead under the coroner Mr Sutchberry. Dr Wilson said that death had occurred some four days previously, but he could not reveal the cause of Mrs Warren's demise until certain organs had been returned from analysis. By this time the newspapers had got hold of the facts, and a search was mounted for Hutchinson. A description of 'a man aged forty-one, 5ft 7in. to 5ft 10in. tall, fresh complexion, brown or ginger hair, grey eyes, wearing a grey suit and heavy black boots, no hat or coat and carrying an attaché case', was circulated to several police forces. There were inevitably reports of mis-sightings and men unfortunate enough to bear a similarity to Hutchinson being wrongly pursued.

The real man was apprehended at Southend on 15 September, thanks to a tip-off from Scotland Yard to the Essex police. They surrounded a boarding house in Broadway Market, near the Southend railway station, where a couple who had booked in were identified as Hutchinson and Doris Dew of Kennington, London, a streetwalker. Hutchinson was taken to Southend police station by Detective Inspector Harris, and was told he would be transferred to Maidenhead where Inspector Barrett wished to interview him in connection with Gwen's murder. At this, he turned to Harris and admitted that he knew the woman and used to live with her, 'but surely the police don't expect I did it.'

At Maidenhead he gave a full statement to Inspector Barrett. He admitted that:

... last Saturday afternoon we had one or two sharp words about the cause I wasn't in work and as regards money coming in; but before 10 p.m. we were quite friendly again except for one thing and that was that she was not going to sleep in the same bed as me any more until I did get work.

They had also argued about his heavy smoking, which irritated her. By bedtime they had made up their differences, and he had been in bed for a while when she came in and took off her nightdress. He thought she was teasing him, until she told him that she had no intention of sharing his bed. He told her to please herself, and went off to sleep. At about midnight he awoke and heard her footsteps going downstairs. Later he added that he thought she had another lover, as he had found a stranger's hat downstairs. On the Sunday morning he made a cup of tea, went into the front bedroom, saw her stockinged feet protruding from under several mattresses, pulled them up and saw that she was dead. Somebody had been in the house, and he thought it must have been either her lover or her ex-husband, whom he alleged, had been making threats against her for some time. He panicked, and instead of reporting her death to the police, he had told a false story to the neighbours, namely that she was still in bed. Although he knew he had been foolish, this did not make him a murderer.

The inquest was opened on 16 September and adjourned for six weeks, and Hutchinson was charged at Maidenhead Police Court with the murder of Gwendoline Anne Warren between 10 and 14 September. When asked by the magistrate, Lieutenant-Colonel Simpson, if he had anything to say, Hutchinson answered that he was not guilty. He was remanded in Oxford Gaol until 23 September. Formal identification of the body was carried out by Thomas Warren. At this time it was considered that he might have been the murderer himself, having lost his wife to another man, particularly if Hutchinson's protestations of innocence proved correct.

The next hearing at Maidenhead Police Court on the 23rd lasted only two minutes, and Hutchinson was remanded in custody for another week. At a subsequent appearance on 4 October he was committed for trial at Reading Assizes the following week. He continued to plead not guilty.

Mr G.R. Paling appeared for the prosecution, and the defence was conducted by Mr Woodward from High Wycombe. The trial included some evidence from Dr Wilson, who stated that Gwen had been struck on the head with a blunt instrument, but this had not been the cause of death and had merely stunned her. She had been killed through asphyxiation caused by a heavy pile of bedding and bedstead items on top of her face and body. In Ronnie's bedroom, under the discarded bedclothes noted by Miss Fleet when she was checking the house with him, Dr Wilson had found a hammer which fitted the description of the blunt instrument used to attack the victim. It was considered most likely, though as yet unproven, that the murder had been committed on the night of Saturday 10 September or early the following morning.

Sir Bernard Spilsbury, the Home Office pathologist, concurred with Dr Wilson's conclusions, and stated that the victim's fingernails were vivid, a common sign of asphyxiation. His autopsy had discovered bruises on the head, which were probably inflicted a few minutes before death. Soon afterwards Hutchinson was formally charged and committed to Reading Assizes on 14 October.

The trial before Mr Justice McKinnon opened on 14 October. For the prosecution was Mr W.G. Earengey KC, while the defence was handled by Mr St John-Micklethwaite, assisted by Mr Cockburn. Mr Warren said he no longer had any interest in his wife's goings-on, but he did not bear her any malice. He had lived with her at 4 Court View, Maidenhead, until 10 June that year, when she took the children and left him. In reply to a question from the prosecution, he stated that Hutchinson had come to him as a lodger in July 1930, and that he believed Connie was Hutchinson's daughter and not his. He had a foolproof alibi for the night of the murder, had never deliberately approached his wife, and considered himself well rid of her.

Mr and Mrs Hutton had both noticed Albert Davis, the second-hand dealer from Bridge Street, at the house on 12 September when he came to collect the goods he had purchased from Hutchinson. The latter had explained this away by saying that he was selling furniture to raise rent money. Mr Hutton testified to the victim's anxieties and fears, and of not being able to sleep properly through worry, as well as his conversation with the accused in the back garden when Hutchinson claimed Gwen was still in bed.

Telling evidence from the prosecution came from William Miles, another neighbour who lived at No. 7, which shared a wall with Davyholme. He said that on the night of 10 September, around 11 p.m., he heard raised voices quarrelling, and after they had stopped, a scraping noise, as if a chair or heavy object was being dragged along the floor. Mr Earengey suggested that this latter noise might have been caused by a person moving one bed over another.

Next to give evidence was Doris Dew, who gave her address as 1 Oakden Street, Kensington Road, London. Identifying herself as a domestic servant, she said a female friend of hers introduced her to Hutchinson at the York Hotel in Waterloo, where she met him at about 6 p.m. on 14 September. He said his name was Ernest and he was going to Southend to check some farm stock. She agreed to go with him, and they booked into rooms at Broadway Market as husband and wife. He had given her a yellow silk jumper and two necklaces, which had since been identified as Mrs Warren's property. The following morning, over breakfast, she read the newspaper and saw the description of a man wanted in connection with a murder at Maidenhead. She read it out to him, remarking that it sounded just like him. His sole response, she said, was a non-committal 'Ugh'. She also spoke of her shock at Hutchinson's arrest the next day.

Next she confirmed that when they met at the hotel, he took a piece of paper from his pocket, tore a strip off, wrote his address on it and passed it to her so that she could write her address on the other piece for him to keep. The prosecution had been given these two pieces of paper as evidence, and when pieced together, they revealed on the back part of a draft letter that had presumably been intended for Thomas Warren. It mentioned that 'the letter from Gwen is useless as I am staying at home as I won't go. I am telling you this because the baby is mine ... Don't come down here under any conditions, whatever else there will be trouble ...

she is hard to get on with.' Warren had not received any letter from his estranged wife, nor any from Hutchinson. It was suspected that the letter might hold a clue as to why Hutchinson and Gwen Wareen could no longer live together, and that he had realised that the only solution was to get her out of the way. The prosecution believed as much, and Earengey said, 'It might suggest that on the Saturday, this woman had written to her husband as she had decided not to live with the prisoner and that, in consequence of her decision, there was a serious quarrel, which, in the end, resulted in her death.'

In his written statement made on the Friday of his arrest, Hutchinson had implied that somebody else entered the house and murdered Gwen. He admitted to having had 'sharp words' with her during the afternoon, and also that she had refused to sleep with him that night and went to the spare room, but then inferred that they were both 'quite friendly again'.

In his statement Hutchinson continued:

> I went off to sleep then, and, just after midnight or between 12 p.m. and 1 a.m., I heard someone go downstairs and guessed it was her. Some time after, I heard someone come back. I did not look out to see who it was. On Sunday morning between six and half-past, I went down to get a cup of tea – made the tea, and brought it back upstairs. I drunk some of my own and went to look for her, as I had made a cup of tea for her and some biscuits for the baby. I looked in the back room where the boy usually sleeps and did not see anyone. I then went into the spare front bedroom, and as soon as I got into the room I thought something was wrong because the bedstead and spare mattress were all put on top of this other bed. I inspected this other bed and pulled the cover up at the far end near the chimney and I could see some stockinged feet. I looked further along and I could see there was a dead woman there, which I recognised in a minute, so I simply put the things back just as I found them when I lifted the cover up, came out and shut the door.

He also said he knew Mrs Warren had received letters from her husband threatening that he would do all the injury to her he could, 'so I do not know whether he done it or not.' Inspector Barrett had collected twenty-one letters and cards from Mr Warren to his estranged wife, but none contained any kind of threat.

Another discrepancy regarding Hutchinson's statement was brought up by the prosecution, who asked how someone could possibly have entered the house and moved the bed and bedding on top of Mrs Warren, without his having heard anything at all. In his statement Hutchinson claimed to have heard somebody going downstairs and upstairs, yet he apparently did not hear anything that would indicate Mrs Warren was being attacked in one room, and then bedding taken from another room being piled on top of her before her attacker left the house.

Hutchinson had also revealed in his statement that on the Monday, after he had put the children on to the bus for Farnham Common and knowing their mother was dead, he went back to Heywood Park, had dinner 'and just messed about the house and outside until the evening,' when he went to the cinema until about 9.30. That night he said he had slept soundly at 8 Heywood Avenue.

At this point the judge intervened to ask him whether he had slept soundly that night. He replied that he had. 'You knew all the while that this poor woman was lying dead under all this stuff?' Hutchinson replied that he knew she was there on the Sunday morning, but did not know what to do for the best. He claimed that he had actually set off to notify the police, and borrowed a bicycle from William Miles at No. 7, but on arriving at Taplow realised that the baby was alone in the house, and had to return. Mr Miles confirmed that Hutchinson had indeed borrowed the bicycle on Sunday morning in an attempt to cycle to Birmingham to see Mrs Warren, but had only got as far as Taplow.

The prosecution then realised they had one unanswerable question. Mrs Warren, with whom he had lived for some months, was lying dead in the house, but he did not know what to do. Whereas any normal person would have gone straight to the police, instead Hutchinson had told a neighbour that she had gone to Birmingham. 'Why did you not go to the police?' asked Earengey.

'I was upset,' replied Hutchinson.

In a further interjection which might have been seen as breaking the bounds of impartiality, the judge intervened to ask, 'Were you so upset that you could sell her furniture and pick up a prostitute in London?' Hutchinson remained silent. When asked a second time why he did not tell the police, he said it was their duty to find out their own jobs. 'I am not a lover of the police.' Such an admission, however truthful it may have been, was hardly calculated to improve his position.

The trial was then adjourned until Saturday morning, 15 October. The defence maintained that the prosecution had not satisfied the court that the murder actually took place in the house, and they had not established beyond all reasonable doubt that it was Hutchinson who had attacked the deceased. Mr Micklethwaite also contended that it was possible a tussle had taken place with somebody, during which Mrs Warren fell, and that was how she died. No motive for murder, he said, had been revealed. The jury were not there to try Hutchinson for being a liar or a coward, but to establish whether he had murdered Gwendoline Anne Warren. In his opinion, this had not been done.

In summing up, the judge pointed out that death had taken place on the night of 10/11 September, and the prosecution contended that it was murder. He then went on to say that on the day when Hutchinson knew she was dead, he had lied to everybody about the circumstances, telling relatives and neighbours she had gone to Birmingham, telling another neighbour she was still in bed, selling her furniture and then going to London, obtaining the services of a prostitute to whom he gave some of Gwen's effects. He also reminded the jury of Hutchinson's

DECLARATION OF SHERIFF

AND OTHERS

(31 Vict. Cap. 24)

We, the undersigned, hereby declare that

Judgement of Death was this Day executed on

ERNEST HUTCHINSON in His Majesty's Prison of

OXFORD in our presence.

Dated this **23rd** day of NOVEMBER 1932

G H Palmer Sheriff of BERKSHIRE

_____ Justice of the Peace

_____ for _____

LCW Richards Governor of the said Prison.

DK Shather-Hunt Chaplain of the said Prison.

The sheriff's declaration of the execution of Ernest Hutchinson.

opening statement when first detained, namely that, 'As they were bound to get me sooner or later, I decided to have as good a time as possible.' The only other possible suspect, he said, was the woman's estranged husband, Thomas Warren, who had made it clear he no longer cared about his wife's activities and therefore had no reason to kill her.

His summing up ended at 1.45 p.m., and the jury were out for seventy minutes. They returned a verdict of guilty. As the death sentence was passed, Hutchinson gave a hollow laugh.

On 15 November an appeal was heard on the grounds that the judge had misdirected the jury and that certain questions contravened the 1898 Criminal Evidence Act, but it was dismissed. Hutchinson spent his last days at Oxford Gaol, and was hanged on the morning of 23 November 1932 by Alfred Allen of Wolverhampton, officiating for the first time. Allen was a one-eyed former provost sergeant, and member of firing squads for deserters during the First World War.

The murder gave the area an unsavoury reputation. A local building firm, Cripps & Green, had recently built a new estate of forty-six houses and found that the adverse publicity had resulted in a disappointing lack of interest. Shortly afterwards the name of the location was changed from Heywood Park to Woodlands Park.

23

A PAIR OF TWEEZERS

Winkfield, 1939

Eighty-five-year-old Frederick Paul, a market gardener, was one of the great characters of Winkfield. Originally from Weymouth, he had settled in the village about thirty years earlier. A widower, he lived alone in a small wooden bungalow consisting of one room, the roof over the other two rooms having long since collapsed. Making his living in an adjacent nursery, he spent most of the day tending his crops, or selling them in Winkfield and surrounding villages, and delivering flowers and plants from his horse-drawn van. Happy in his solitary existence, he lived simply, slept in an armchair, and never wanted for anything more. It was rumoured that he had a substantial amount of cash hidden away on the premises. That, and the fact that he lived alone, made him vulnerable.

On 8 February 1939 Frederick Godfrey, the postman, delivered a letter to the nursery at about 7 a.m. and stayed to chat for a few minutes. As ever he found Fred very friendly. Two days later he came to make another delivery to the nursery, but could get no reply. There was nothing unusual in this, as Fred was often up and about very early.

That night, between 11 and 11.30 p.m., William Coombs, a farm labourer from Crouch Lane, Winkfield, heard the sound of gunshots coming from the direction of the Tally Ho public house, very close to Mr Paul's nursery. As it was a rural district with plenty of large estates, poachers and gamekeepers, this was hardly surprising. On 10 February Mr Godfrey had no deliveries for the nursery. A local newspaper boy pushed Fred's paper through the door of the bungalow at about 7.30 a.m. but noticed nothing amiss. However, about three hours later Albert Gray, the butcher's roundsman, delivered some meat. The door was ajar, and Gray pushed it a little further so that he could place the order inside. He saw the room was in a mess, with drawers pulled out and letters and papers scattered over the floor. On the wall in the corner were traces of spattered blood, and a pool of blood on the threadbare carpet. Even so, Gray still placed his order on the table, then closed the door and

 left without making any further inspection, or even notifying the authorities. At about 12.15 p.m., Reg Stone, a coalman on his deliver round, made a further inspection after he noticed lamps alight at that time of day. After seeing the disarray inside, he notified the Winkfield police.

Constable Coombs arrived at the nursery at 1 p.m., made his way through the debris of the one-roomed dwelling, and concluded that it had been ransacked by somebody making a frenzied search, rather than mere vandalism. The bloodstains and a pair of broken glasses were further proof of foul play, with further stains and scuffed grass stretching from the back of the dwelling to a shallow pool, a distance of about 80 yards. There he found the submerged body of Frederick Paul, with only the head and shoulders visible above the murky surface. His skull and part of his neck had been blasted away.

He sent for assistance and within an hour Superintendent Braby arrived from Wokingham, accompanied by several constables. Mr Paul's body was taken indoors, fully clothed except for a jacket. The hip pocket of his trousers had been pulled out, and the other pockets between them contained 4s 8d in change.

One of Braby's first actions was to have the shallow pool pumped dry. This revealed the jacket, which had been turned inside out and evidently thoroughly searched for cash. No weapon came to light, but beside the pool was a damp patch of blood, which was assumed to be where the murderer left the body to rest briefly before throwing it into the water. Two cartridge wads were also found close by. The police thought Mr Paul may have had heard suspicious noises and gone out to investigate.

At midday on 11 February the body was examined by Dr James Vernon of Ascot. He announced that Paul had been shot twice, once in the temple and once in the neck, and either shot would have proved fatal.

An inquest was held on 14 February at Ascot police station before Mr R.S. Payne of Reading. Evidence produced endorsed the view that it was definitely a case of murder. The body was identified by Walter Paul, the victim's son, who said that his father possessed no firearms. Dr Vernon placed the time of death at between 10 p.m. and midnight on 9 February, based on the temperature and state of the body. The murder was assumed to have taken place at night as the lamps in the bungalow were still alight, and William Coombs's evidence of hearing shots from that direction at between 11 and 11.30 p.m. was accepted as the time of death. Superintendent Braby informed the court that inquiries were proceeding well and he hoped there would be a preliminary hearing soon. The proceedings were adjourned until 9 March, with the coroner directing that the body should be taken to the Royal Berkshire Hospital.

On the evening of 14 February, Superintendent Braby and Constable Coombs arrested George Henry Willis, a twenty-nine-year-old labourer, at his home at

Windsor Guildhall. (© Kenneth Allen, Omagh)

No. 5 Braiswick Cottages, Ascot. Protesting his innocence, Willis was taken to Ascot police station. The police took several items from his home including rubber gloves, a 4.10 shotgun, a quantity of shot, powder, wadding and cartridge cases, and a pair of tweezers.

Willis appeared at a court at the police station the next day, before Mr A.P. Shaw, still pleading his innocence, and was remanded until the preliminary hearing. This was opened on 10 March at Windsor Guildhall, where there was no dock, so Willis spent the entire proceedings sitting on an open bench alongside various other people involved in the case. Again Mr Shaw presided, with the prosecution represented by Mr G.R. Paling, and the defence by Mr E.R. Guest. Superintendent Braby described in detail the finding of the body, the arrest, and the items removed from Willis's home. The powder and wadding he had removed were very similar to those found at the scene of the crime. Willis evidently made his own ammunition from components manufactured by ICI, which were identical to those found at the nursery.

When Willis was questioned on the matter, said Braby, he said he had bought the ammunition from a Mr Ayres at Easthampstead, something which the latter man denied. Willis was then asked whether he had been near Winkfield, and he said he had not been there for over a year, but Ayres told the police that he and Willis often took a shortcut through Winkfield on their way to Bracknell.

Next, Braby went on to describe the odd jobs done by Willis for Mr Paul. He was familiar with the layout of the tiny residence, and was also well aware that Fred kept cash in his hip pocket. Braby also stated that witnesses had heard Willis mention in local pubs that Paul had a 'long stocking', or a good deal of money hidden away.

The superintendent then mentioned other aspects of the case. A butler and a boot boy from Foliejon Park had seen Willis near the nursery on 9 February. Later Mr Paling produced the butler and asked him to point out the man he had seen. At this the defence objected, and the objection was upheld. The Superintendent told the inquiry that Willis had no alibi for 9 February, other than that he had been at home in bed. At last he spoke about the tweezers, which had been found among a load of clock parts at 5 Braiswick Cottages, belonging to Mr Paul, and he would prove that they had been in the deceased's possession shortly before the murder. They were unusual because one blade had been broken, filed and then flattened.

His evidence was followed by that of Walter Paul. He said his father used to carry some of his money in a small seed packet kept in his hip pocket. A detective said he had found eight £1 notes in a seed packet in one of the trouser pockets. Walter also said he recognised the tweezers as belonging to his father, and that he had often heard Willis's statement that his father had 'a long stocking'.

Willis was next to speak. He said he had known Mr Paul for several years and had done odd jobs for him like ratting and cutting peasticks, but had been near the nursery for over two years. He admitted that he and Ayres had sometimes walked through Winkfield en route to Bracknell. He also said that he did not make his own ammunition, and if he had not purchased it from Ayres then he did so from one of the other local suppliers. ICI components were widely used. When asked about his references to Mr Paul's 'long stocking', he said he never used this expression and had not mentioned it in the pubs – and certainly not in front of Walter Paul. In addition he claimed that the two men who claimed to have seen him in the neighbourhood of Tally Ho Lane at 5 p.m. on 9 February were mistaken. Moreover, the tweezers had been in his possession since 1932, and were given to him with a load of old clock parts by a Mrs Norton of Binfield.

His reason for not having an alibi, he said, was because he was innocent and he did not think he really needed one. On the evening of 8 February a Miss Rapley had come to see him from Fifield. They talked for a while, and she took the bus home at about 8.30 p.m. Willis cycled after it, and they had chatted again nearer her home, after which he cycled home about 10.30 p.m. and went to bed. On 9 February he had spent the day gardening, finishing at about 5 p.m., then walked to the Stag and Hounds at Braywick, returning home at 8.30 p.m. and going to bed. The inquiry decided to remand him to Reading Assizes.

The trial was held on 14 May 1939 at Reading Assizes, and lasted two days. Mr Justice Charles presided, with Mr W.H. Cartwright-Sharp KC and Mr H.H. Madocks for the prosecution, and Mr A.J. Long KC and Mr Guest for the defence.

In addition to the evidence already given, additional information now came to light. Mr Arthur Dunsford, butler at Foliejon Park, said that at 5 p.m. on 9 February the telephone was out of order, so his mistress had asked him to cycle to South Lodge. On his journey he dismounted to cross a cattle grid when he saw a man with a haggard expression standing there. He said hello to the man, who did not answer. This same person, he said, was the prisoner in the dock. The boot boy, who had followed the butler with a further message, also witnessed and recognised the prisoner. When Mr Long asked him if he was sure it was the same man, Dunsford replied that he was certain. 'At twilight time, on a drizzly night, with only a fleeting glimpse as you passed him by. Can you be certain this is the man?' asked Long. The reply was a rather less confident yes the second time.

Next on the stand was Dr G. Roche-Lynch, a ballistics expert, who said that the bullets that had been taken from the body were made of a particularly soft lead identical to the lead found in 5 Braywick Cottages. Mr Long asked if this was not lead of a common type found all over the country, but the doctor answered that it was unusual. He also drew attention to the tweezers, saying they were unusual as well. Later, John Norton of Binfield identified the tweezers as a pair his mother had given Willis seven years earlier, at the same time as some watch and clock pieces. They had been in his mother's possession for many years previously.

Mr Cartwright-Sharp asked Willis how long the tweezers had been in his possession, and Willis told him since 1932. He said he could not explain how they matched a pair that Mr Paul possessed shortly before he died, and when asked how the blade became broken, he said they were broken when they were given to him. How did it become beaten and flattened was the next question.

'I did it myself, I used them as a screwdriver for watch repairs,' was Willis's confident answer. He then explained that he did not have a small enough screwdriver, so he made himself one. Cartwright-Sharp then asked him to demonstrate how he used them. To the court's amazement, as the clerk handed the prisoner an open-backed watch, Willis took the tweezers in his right hand, removed three tiny screws from the back of the watch, and placed them on the dock without hesitation.

Cartwright-Sharp's speech remarked on several coincidences in the case. He asked the jury if they did not find it remarkable that the cartridges, lead and wadding were the same, and he thought it had been proved that the tweezers were the same. Why, he asked, had Willis lied about purchasing the ammunition from Ayres, and why had he no alibi? Was it right that so many unfortunate coincidences had been experienced by one man?

In Mr Long's view, the prosecution had failed to establish anything. Bodies immersed in water could give very varied indications as to the time of death. William Coombs's gunshots could easily have been fired by poachers, and the court was not even sure of the precise date of Mr Paul's death. He had been beaten before he died, and was probably lying on the ground when he was shot; probably with a revolver of the same bore as that used by Willis, but it was quite a common model. The eyewitnesses' testimony was unreliable as it was nearly dark and raining at the time, they had only the most fleeting of glimpses, and they could only place the person they had seen somewhere near Tally Ho Lane on one of the days in question. There must have been several people in the area. Willis had had the tweezers in his possession for several years, as he had proved by his ability to perform such a delicate operation with them. It was therefore unlikely that the murderer would stop to pick up a small cheap pair of broken tweezers and carry them about with him, thus incriminating himself.

In his summing up, Mr Justice Charles described the case as the most brutal he had come across in his eleven years on the bench. He had been impressed by Willis's dexterity with the tweezers, and had to ask the jury directly whether a man could have committed such an abhorrent crime and then, in a crowded courtroom, while on trial for his life, used implements owned by the deceased man without a trace of emotion.

The jury retired for fifteen minutes before returning a verdict of not guilty.

24

'I DID NOT FIGURE IN SUCH A MURDER'

Maidenhead, 1948

During the last years of the nineteenth century, the future Mrs Minnie Freeman-Lee was a noted beauty and socialite. It was said that she had been the toast of parties and receptions in fashionable places such as Vienna, Paris, Rome and Monte Carlo. At around this time she married a barrister; they had a son, and settled in England. By 1908 they had moved to Maidenhead, where they lived in Wynford, a redbrick house in Ray Park Avenue with seventeen rooms.

Mr and Mrs Freeman-Lee lost their son in the First World War, and Mr Freeman-Lee died not long afterwards. Nevertheless, in widowhood Mrs Freeman-Lee clung stubbornly to her independence. There was no family left to advise her what she ought to do, and any suggestions from the council or kindly neighbours, or indeed the daily meals-on-wheels helpers, that she might consider moving to a smaller, more manageable property, or even a residential home where she would be well cared for, were met with a firm refusal. She was determined to see out her remaining days in her once magnificent but now sadly deteriorating house. By 1948 the elderly recluse, whose age was variously given as eighty-eight or ninety-four, was just living in a front lounge. Every other room in the rest of the property was stacked from floor to ceiling with disintegrating antique furniture and clutter under a leaking roof.

Apart from any pension or savings she may have accrued, her sole income was £6 a week from a benevolent society. Sometimes she would allow herself lunch at the Thames Hotel nearby, venturing out slowly with her walking stick. A stroke had left her with little movement in one hand, but somehow she still managed on her own most of the time. She was said to smoke forty cigarettes a day, which she always collected from the local shop herself. Naturally, any elderly recluse in the neighbourhood was assumed to be wealthy, and bound to be the subject of speculation about piles of cash stored on the premises.

On 1 June 1948 her milkman, George Rome, noticed that she had not taken in her previous day's delivery. This was the first time he had ever known her to leave milk on the doorstep for twenty-four hours, so he asked one of her neighbours, Arthur Hilsdon, if he had seen her. The latter had not, so they both knocked on the front door. As there was no reply, they pushed it open – Mrs Freeman-Lee generally left the door unlocked – and walked in. They found the house in an even worse mess than usual, and it looked as if it had recently been ransacked. The two men went round every room in turn, calling out her name, but received no answer. What they did find was her bunch of keys on the landing, and a black court shoe nearby, one of a pair which she wore all the time.

They notified the police at once, and Constable George Langton joined them., but he failed to find anything else. Next they contacted Mrs Freeman-Lee's solicitor, Kenneth Ruffe-Thomas, who lived a few doors along the road. The men had decided that he was probably the elderly lady's main point of contact, and would certainly have been told if she was going away, though at her time of life and in her frail condition, she was most unlikely to venture further than the shops or the hotel. Ruffe-Thomas was not aware of any plans she might have made, but once he arrived at the house he cast his eyes around for anything which might provide a clue.

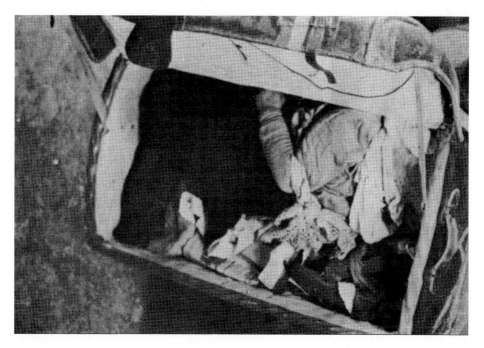

The body of Minnie Freeman-Lee, discovered by her solicitor, Kenneth Ruffe-Thomas, at her house.

Above left: *Oxford Gaol, closed in 1996, is now a shopping and heritage complex, with the Malmaison Oxford. (© Terry Bean, Beanwebs and Beandesigns)*

Above right: *Reading Crown Court, Shire Hall. (© R. Sones)*

By sheer chance he saw a battered old trunk in the hall. It was not locked, and he started to undo the fastenings. To his horror, once it was open it revealed the body of the poor woman.

He called for Constable Langton, who brought in more police officers, and the area was cordoned off. Next to be brought on the case was Superintendent W.J. Crombie of Reading CID, assisted by Superintendent W.H. Benstead of Maidenhead. Crombie made enquiries and found that the last person to see Mrs Freeman-Lee alive was an electrician, who had done some repairs for her and left at about 6.20 p.m. on Saturday 29 May. Death had evidently occurred between that time and the discovery of the body on the morning of 1 June.

Pathologist Dr Keith Simpson was called in, and, after inspecting the body on the following afternoon, he concluded that death had occurred about forty-eight hours previously. Her head was badly bruised, but not enough to kill her, despite ill-founded speculation in the newspapers that she had been 'bludgeoned to death'. The most likely cause of death was thought to have been asphyxia. She had been beaten around the head, her hands had been tied behind her back with a woolen shawl, and she had been gagged with a towel. She had then been crammed into the trunk while still alive, and left to suffocate. The gag had become congested with mucus and saliva, thus gradually preventing her from being able to breathe.

On 3 June officers from Scotland Yard arrived, including Superintendent Chapman of the Flying Squad, Detective Sergeant Hislop, and Chief Superintendent Frederick Cherrill, regarded as the Yard's greatest expert on fingerprinting. The latter's initial searches drew a blank, until he was sifting through the dead woman's bedding. Her makeshift bed was in the corner of the room downstairs which she used all the time, and on it he found a 2in-square, lidless jewellery box. The lid turned up underneath the bed, had been trodden on and was squashed flat. He brushed it with fingerprint dust and it revealed two faint fragments of prints. Taking it to his colleague at the Yard, Chief Inspector Holten, both men immediately matched them with those of George Russell, an itinerant Irish labourer who had had a police record since being arrested for theft at Oxford in 1933.

Forty-five-year-old Russell was traced to a hotel at St Albans within a week and arrested. At the time he had with him a blue silk scarf, which was identified as the property of Minnie Freeman-Lee. He said that he had bought it for 1s from a man at a hostel in London. Enquiries around Maidenhead revealed that he had been well known there as a jobbing gardener, when he had been pulled in by the police for various small misdemeanours, and he had also worked on a casual basis at a hotel in Maidenhead.

Chapman took Russell to Wynford for questioning, acting on the theory that if an accused man is confronted by the scene of the crime he will either give way or break down completely. When questioned about his fingerprints and the scarf, Russell burst into tears. Nevertheless, he did not admit to the murder, only saying that he had once called at the house to offer to do some gardening. He was remanded in Oxford Gaol pending the Reading Assizes in October.

At the two-day trial, held on 15 and 16 October, he appeared before Mr Justice Hallett. Ironically, at this trial Keith Simpson observed that the judge had on his desk two volumes of *Russell on Crime*.

The prosecution contended that Russell had entered the house with intent to steal, been disturbed by Mrs Freeman-Lee, hit her on the head, tied her up, threw her in the trunk and left her to die. When Russell was questioned, he as good as convicted himself with the statement, 'Did I murder this poor aged woman for something she was supposed to have, but had not? No, I did not figure in such a murder.' How, everyone asked, could Russell know the deceased had nothing unless he had searched the room, expecting to find something?

In his summing up, the judge informed the jury that if an intruder was to use violence on his victim while executing that intrusion, and if that violence was to result in the death of the victim, then as a point of law this should be regarded as murder. He continued:

> You have to take your choice on a question of credibility between believing that Russell has lied, or that Superintendent Chapman and his colleagues have told a series of very wicked lies. You may think this man has been the victim, if he is innocent, of a number of cruel circumstances. He was in the hostel just at the wrong time, and bought just the wrong thing – the scarf, and on a box in Mrs Lee's room there were not one, but two fingerprints – which Superintendent Cherrill says without the slightest doubt are the fingerprints of this man.

Cherrill's testimony proved conclusive enough. The jury was out for two hours, before returning a verdict of guilty. Russell was sentenced to death. An appeal to the Home Secretary was turned down and he was hanged at Oxford Gaol on 2 December 1948.

BIBLIOGRAPHY

BOOKS

Browne, Douglas, & Tullett, Tom, *Bernard Spilsbury: His life and cases*, Harrap, 1951
Eddleston, John J., *The Encyclopedia of Executions*, John Blake, 2004
Fielding, Steve, *The Hangman's Record, Vol. 1, 1868-1899; Vol. 2, 1900-1929; Vol. 3, 1930-1964*, CBD, 1994-2005
Kidd-Hewitt, David, *Berkshire Tales of Mystery and Murder*, Countryside, 2004
Long, Roger, *Final Commitment: An Anthology of Murder in Old Berkshire*, Alan Sutton/ Berkshire Books, 1994
McLoughlin, Ian, *Berkshire Murders*, Countryside, 1992
Vale, Allison, & Rattle, Alison, *Amelia Dyer: Angel Maker*, Andre Deutsch, 2007

NEWSPAPERS

Belfast Newsletter
Bristol Mercury & Daily Post
Buckinghamshire Herald
Caledonian Mercury
Daily News
Illustrated Police News
Leeds Mercury
Lloyd's Weekly Newspaper
Morning Chronicle
Newcastle Courant
Reading Chronicle
Reynolds' Newspaper
The Times

INTERNET

Newgate Calendar (www.newgatecalendar.co.uk)

INDEX

ALSO BY JOHN VAN DER KISTE

A Divided Kingdom

A Grim Almanac of Cornwall

A Grim Almanac of Devon

Childhood at Court 1819-1914

Cornish Murders (with Nicola Sly)

Cornwall's Own

Crowns in a Changing World

Dearest Affie (with Bee Jordaan)

Dearest Vicky, Darling Fritz

Devon Murders

Edward VII's Children

Emperor Francis Joseph

Frederick III

George III's Children

George V's Children

Gilbert & Sullivan's Christmas

Kaiser Wilhelm II

King George II and Queen Caroline

Kings of the Hellenes

Northern Crowns

Once a Grand Duchess (with Coryne Hall)

Plymouth: History & Guide

Princess Victoria Melita

Queen Victoria's Children

Somerset Murders (with Nicola Sly)

Sons, Servants and Statesmen

Surrey Murders

The Georgian Princesses

The Romanovs 1818-1959

West Country Murders (with Nicola Sly)

William and Mary

Windsor and Habsburg